LIVING BEYOND LIMITS

BEC FEASEY

Living Beyond Limits

First published in Australia in 2026 by Ultra Resilience Publishing

© Bec Feasey 2026

ISBNs
978-1-7644352-9-1 (paperback)
978-1-7644352-8-4 (ebook)
978-1-7644352-7-7 (audiobook)

Cover Design: Tess McCabe
Typeset by Luke Harris, Working Type Books
Printed in Australia

A catalogue record for this book is available from the National Library of Australia

NOTE ON NAMES

Some names in this book have been changed to protect the privacy of individuals, while maintaining the truth of events and relationships. Although these names may not be the real names of the people involved, their roles, connections, and experiences are accurately represented.

For the journey — with its twists and turns,

and the values that guide us.

CONTENTS

INTRODUCTION

For over 20 years, I battled relentless pain, fatigue and nausea that were often dismissed or misunderstood by medical professionals. By the time doctors discovered the cause, the damage was already done. I was diagnosed with stage four (severe) endometriosis – a complex, whole-body condition where tissue similar to the lining of the womb grows in places it doesn't belong, causing widespread pain and inflammation. It can feel as though your entire system needs rewiring – the immune system is dysregulated, nerves are hypersensitive, and the gut–brain axis completely out of sync. My condition was so advanced my abdominal organs were fused together by endometrial tissue.

I felt relieved when I was diagnosed; it hadn't all been in my head. But that relief was mixed with grief and anger – grief for the years of agony and the damage done to my body, and anger toward a medical system that had overlooked my symptoms for far too long.

Living without a diagnosis and being told by some medical professionals that my symptoms were "normal" left me with little choice but to keep moving forward. It was either that or miss out on life. Over time, I learned, often the hard way, how to keep going despite discomfort, how to pace myself, and how to find strength in the small victories.

It was this mindset that eventually drew me to ultra-trail running. Just as I had learned to navigate the unpredictable challenges of chronic illness, I learned to cope with the challenges of endurance running; both demanded the same persistence, patience and mental fortitude. Every long run became a lesson in resilience, every kilometre a reminder that even in the face of pain, the human body and spirit can endure far more than we imagine.

I'm Bec Feasey – a Master of Professional Psychology student, an endurance athlete, and someone who has navigated the highs and lows of chronic illness. I wrote this book not only to share my story, but to share the hard-won lessons that came with it. My hope is that it offers inspiration, practical insights and encouragement to anyone facing their own challenges – whether physical, mental or emotional.

This book is part memoir, part guide, weaving together:

- Personal stories: honest accounts of living with a chronic illness and pursuing ambitious goals.

- Reflections: lessons on mindset, coping and motivation.

- Practical takeaways: strategies to support growth.

While I share approaches that have helped me, this book is not a substitute for professional psychological care. Everyone's journey is unique, and if you're dealing with pain, chronic illness or mental health challenges, I encourage you to seek professional support.

Whatever you're facing right now, I hope this book meets you where you are. My journey has taught me that even in the face of obstacles, growth, strength, and joy are possible.

Let's walk this path together – toward resilience, empowerment and living beyond limits.

PART ONE:

BREAKING POINT

ONE

UNMASKED

DRIVING ON THE FREEWAY AWAY from work, I gripped the steering wheel as hard as I could. The abdominal pain was unbearable – sharp, relentless, consuming. I felt light-headed and nauseous, weighing whether to pull over and call an ambulance. The hospital I was heading to was still some distance away, and as each freeway exit approached, my mind scrambled for options. Stopping felt like a delay I couldn't afford. Even if I called an ambulance, I knew I'd get there faster if I just kept driving. This was a new kind of pain, and I knew it was serious.

That morning, the pain had begun as a dull ache while I was getting ready for work – distinct from the usual discomfort I'd learned to navigate. I took painkillers, a routine part of managing chronic pain, told myself to push through, and mentally prepared for the day ahead. Over the years, I'd learned to break time into small, bearable fragments: *Just make it to lunchtime*, I'd say. On worse days, I'd measure time in half-hour blocks, pushing forward in tiny acts of endurance – so even getting into the car that day felt monumental. The commute – an hour and a half of traffic followed by a twenty-minute walk to the office – loomed like a marathon of its own. When I'm in pain, I prefer solitude;

being around others can be exhausting. The thought of putting on my brave face, of hiding what I was feeling inside, drained me before I'd even left the house. Performing normalcy takes energy, and imagining sustaining it all day was overwhelming. But it was a familiar battle. I'd been here many times before.

I knew I wouldn't be able to sit at my desk quietly and go unnoticed. There were meetings to attend, emails to write, phone calls to make, colleagues asking questions, and project deadlines to meet, in a fast-paced environment. That morning, on the drive to work, my mind was flooded with a single thought: *I can't do this.* I found myself arguing silently: *Just turn around, you're not well,* versus *You can't let your colleagues or manager down; just keep going.* The debate went back and forth. After years of living with chronic pain, I had somehow learned to catch these unhelpful thoughts and replace them with more constructive ones. It was the only way I knew how to cope – the only way to keep moving forward. I managed to shift my thinking: *I can do this. I'm strong. I've managed it before, and I'll get through today too.* That small internal pivot didn't erase the pain or fatigue, but it gave me just enough strength to take the next step in the right direction. I took pride in my work and in the sense of belonging it gave me. It felt good to know that what I did mattered – that I was part of something bigger than my pain. Moments like that morning drive taught me that perseverance wasn't only about showing up for others, but about showing up for myself.

Years later, as a psychology student, I discovered how our thoughts shape our emotions, and how those emotions, in turn, guide our behaviours. This interconnected cycle – thoughts influencing feelings, feelings influencing actions – is the foundation of Cognitive

Behaviour Therapy (CBT). If I had stayed with the thought *I can't do this* every time I was in pain, I would have withdrawn from life, struggled to hold a job, and felt increasingly defeated. But by reframing my thinking and seeing myself with more balance and compassion, I could regain a sense of accomplishment and purpose. When learning CBT, something clicked: I had been practising this skill intuitively my entire adult life. Even now, I'm not entirely sure how I learned it – perhaps out of necessity, perhaps out of resilience – but it became one of my most valuable tools for survival and growth.

I made it to work and went through the usual pleasantries with my colleagues and manager – no one suspected a thing. That's exactly how I wanted it. I didn't want sympathy. I didn't want to have to tell them every time I wasn't feeling well or explain why my body was working against me. I just wanted to carry on as if nothing were wrong.

But by mid-morning, the pain had intensified beyond measure. I sat at my desk, trying to focus, trying to hide it. Internalising pain had become second nature. Over the years, I'd mastered small coping strategies at work – invisible to others – such as digging my nails into my thigh under the desk, biting the inside of my cheek to redirect the pain, or slipping away for a few minutes to double over in private, release the mask, and just breathe through it. That day, though, my tactics failed. The pain was all-consuming. Quietly, I turned to a colleague and said, "I'm not well – I need to go."

The pain was excruciating. My mind raced as I walked to the car, weighing my options. I had two choices: go to the Royal Melbourne Hospital, close to work, or drive to a hospital closer to home. Seeing a GP was out of the question – I was far beyond that point. I briefly considered the inconvenience it would cause my partner, Mark, if I went to the Royal Melbourne Hospital, since it's an hour from where we live. In the end, I chose to drive to a hospital closer to home.

I was hunched over, moaning in pain, gripping the steering wheel as the agony rippled through me. Desperation began to creep in. Every red light felt endless, every kilometre stretched impossibly long. To keep myself going, I broke the journey into fragments, offering myself reassurance: *Just 40 more minutes. Hang in there. You'll get help soon. You'll get more pain relief.*

At the emergency department, I was told to wait. The room was full. I can't remember how long it took before I was seen – the pain had dulled slightly by then – but what I do remember is the lack of compassion. A male doctor began asking me very personal medical questions aloud, right there in the waiting room, in front of strangers. I felt embarrassed, dismissed, and demoralised. My pain was treated flippantly.

"The only pain that extreme is likely kidney stones," he said. I explained that I'd had kidney stones years earlier, and while that pain had been extreme, this felt different. He didn't believe me. The dismissal was familiar – almost expected. For years, I'd sat in doctors' rooms describing my pain: the kind that had me crippled on the floor at 3 am; the kind that left me crouched over in the bathroom at work and at home; the kind that would ache for hours or hit me like a freight train out of nowhere. Not one medical professional ever took it seriously. Maybe they thought I was exaggerating. Maybe they thought I was weak, overly sensitive, or simply hormonal. Maybe they just didn't know how to recognise the symptoms of endometriosis. I had raised the possibility of endometriosis once or twice, only to be told it was highly unlikely.

I remember one GP visit clearly. I was worried that a strong painkiller I relied on was being taken off the shelves and made prescription-only. I didn't want to beg for medication every month. I had my own strategy for managing pain – I avoided tablets unless it reached a five out of ten and I could no longer think straight. But when I explained this, the GP waved it off. He told me the pain I was describing was "normal female pain" and that it was because I hadn't yet been pregnant. I respect doctors, but that moment – and countless others like it – left me defeated. I had done everything I was supposed to do: sought help, described my symptoms, persisted. Each time, I walked away feeling let down. Still, deep down, I knew something wasn't right. My female friends didn't experience pain like this. The more I was dismissed, the more I began to doubt myself. Maybe I was weak. Maybe it really was all in my head.

Once I was admitted to emergency, tests followed – scans, physical exams, endless questions. The pain was concentrated on the right side of my abdomen, and soon there was concern my appendix had ruptured, despite nothing showing on the scans. Hours later, I was prepped for surgery to have it removed.

When I woke, nauseous and vomiting from the anaesthetic, a female doctor pulled the curtain around my bed. "Your appendix was fine," she said. "We removed it anyway – you don't really need it – but it looks like you might have endometriosis. There was blood in your abdomen. You had an endometrioma on your right ovary, and it ruptured."

An endometrioma, often called a chocolate cyst, is a type of ovarian cyst that forms when endometrial tissue grows inside the ovary. Each month, this trapped tissue responds to hormonal changes, bleeding internally, with nowhere for the blood to go. Over time, the old blood collects and thickens into a dark, tar-like fluid, giving the cyst its distinctive name. Endometriomas can cause severe pelvic pain, bloating, and inflammation, and when they rupture, the contents spill into the abdominal cavity, triggering intense pain and inflammation. They're a common feature of advanced endometriosis and often signal that the disease has spread beyond the womb, affecting nearby organs and tissues.

That day, the truth revealed itself in the harshest way possible. A ruptured endometrioma had finally forced my body to be heard. In the chaos of emergency and a mistaken appendicitis diagnosis, the real answer finally emerged: endometriosis. After more than 20 years of uncertainty and dismissal, at the age of 38, I finally had a name for my symptoms. That moment became a turning point – not just for my health, but for how I understood my body, my limits, and my strength.

In the days that followed, I immersed myself in everything I could find about endometriosis, clinging to knowledge as if it were a lifeline. My determination to take charge of my health was fierce. Once I'd recovered from surgery, I booked a GP appointment and insisted on a referral to a specialist I had carefully researched and chosen – Melbourne-based, experienced, and transparent in the information he shared online. I didn't care how the GP perceived me: dramatic, difficult, or wrong. I had spent too many years silencing my instincts to keep the peace. This time, I was done seeking permission to be believed.

When I met with the specialist, he explained that a laparoscopy, keyhole surgery, was required to determine the extent of the disease and provide treatment. Having just recovered from one operation, I hesitated, but I knew it was necessary. I needed answers.

Looking back, that appointment marked more than just another medical step – it became a moment of clarity about my strength, endurance, and the importance of trusting my own instincts. The lessons that followed weren't immediately clear to me then, but they've stayed with me ever since.

Reflections:

* Resilience isn't always loud or dramatic – it lives in the quiet, steadfast act of showing up, one step at a time. Every moment I pushed through pain and fatigue, choosing to be present for friends, family, or work colleagues, I was taking small yet profoundly meaningful steps. They weren't grand gestures, but each one mattered, quietly shaping my strength and endurance over time.

* Learning to trust my instincts has been one of the most powerful lessons of my life. For more than 20 years, I second-guessed the signals my body and mind were sending me, doubting myself in the face of uncertainty or external opinions. Yet, time and time again, I've discovered that those gut feelings – subtle, persistent, and sometimes uncomfortable – were trying to guide me toward the right choice. Trusting my instinct doesn't always make the path easy, but it has taught me to listen closely, to honour my experience, and to take decisive action even when others question it. It's a quiet, steadfast confidence that I carry with me every day, and it has repeatedly proven to be an ally in navigating challenges both big and small.

Practical takeaways:

Breaking time into fragments

Breaking time into small, manageable pieces helps me endure moments that feel overwhelming. What started as a way to cope with pain has evolved into a life skill I draw on in other challenges. Focusing on just one step at a time keeps me moving forward, even when the bigger picture feels too heavy to face.

How I apply it:

- I use half-hour markers to manage pain or challenging moments – focusing only on getting through the next small block of time.

- Using the same principle, I break large overwhelming tasks into smaller, achievable steps. For example, I have a whiteboard as a visual guide for tasks, like planning a holiday – booking flights and accommodation, finding a pet sitter, submitting travel documents, making payments and organising activities. Seeing each step mapped out helps turn chaos into clarity, offering both a sense of direction and accomplishment along the way.

Self-advocacy

Advocating for myself isn't optional – it's essential. In medical appointments, I speak honestly about what I'm feeling and ask questions until I understand. I prepare ahead, stay curious, and trust my instincts: if something feels wrong, it usually is. Over time, this approach has helped me feel more confident and in control, even in situations where it's easy to feel powerless.

How I apply it:

- I prepare questions or notes before appointments, so nothing is missed.

- I speak up if something isn't clear or doesn't feel right.

- I trust my intuition and seek a second opinion when needed.

- I keep medical records for reference to help guide decisions and conversations.

Self-compassion

Instead of feeling guilty or wondering if I could've done more to reach a diagnosis sooner, I've learned to acknowledge the challenges I faced and the ways I coped. I remind myself that I did the best I could with what I knew at the time. Extending compassion toward myself has been just as important as seeking understanding from others – it softens self-blame and allows space for healing.

How I apply it:

- When self-criticism appears, I pause and reframe my thoughts with kindness rather than judgement.

- I reflect on how I coped in the past with gratitude, recognising that survival is its own form of strength.

- I treat myself with the same understanding I'd offer a friend going through something similar.

- I allow rest and emotional space on difficult days without guilt or comparison.

TWO

DIAGNOSIS

I WAS NERVOUS PREPARING FOR SURGERY. Based on prior surgeries, I knew I had a poor tolerance to anaesthetic, frequently suffering nausea and vomiting. Years earlier, after an operation for a broken collarbone, I'd experienced tachycardia – a sudden, rapid heartbeat that raced uncontrollably for hours. A physical pounding that felt as exhausting and overwhelming as sprinting uphill. I remember lying in my hospital bed, anxious and restless, my heart racing in a way that felt unrelenting – a deeply unsettling and uncomfortable sensation. That memory had stayed with me, tucked away but not forgotten.

Before the laparoscopy, I told the anaesthetist about it. He listened carefully, not dismissing my fear as nerves. His calm confidence was reassuring. He met with me beforehand, reviewed my chart, and promised a gold-standard approach focused on careful monitoring and medication tailored to my body. His words stuck. They didn't erase the fear, but they built a bridge of trust. For the first time in a long time, I felt looked after – seen as a person, not just another patient.

But there was another layer to my anxiety, one that ran deeper than the fear of surgery itself. I hated asking for help. Always have.

Growing up, independence was survival – you got things done, no matter what. Accepting care felt like weakness. Mark had already supported me through the appendix surgery, and now I was asking him to do it again – to carry both of us while I healed. We live on a farm, surrounded by horses, paddocks, and the rhythm of work that never pauses. So much of our life depends on physical effort – feeding animals, moving hay, fixing fences. Being unable to do my share left me with gnawing guilt, even though he never once complained. He reassured me, said we'd manage, but guilt doesn't listen to logic. It always lingers, stubborn and sharp.

In the days before surgery, I busied myself with preparation – changing the bed sheets, cleaning the house, writing lists of horse-feed rotations and small chores. It was my way of trying to control something in a situation where so much felt uncontrollable.

When the day finally arrived, I sat alone in the hospital lounge, the sterile smell of disinfectant in the air, underscored by the distant murmur of voices and the rhythmic beeping of monitors somewhere down the corridor. My nerves grew stronger with each passing minute. What if they didn't find anything – what if it wasn't endometriosis after all? What if it was something else, something worse? And what if they did find it – and it was severe? The unknown felt unbearably heavy. I tried to calm my mind, breathing slowly, reminding myself that whatever they found, I'd finally have answers. The worry never really disappeared, but I made space for it – accepting that fear was part of the process, not a sign of weakness.

When my name was called, I changed into a gown, surgical cap, compression socks and booties. I took a quick selfie for Mark just for a laugh, told him I loved him, and then waited. The nurse showed me to my bed and brought me a warm blanket – small mercy, but it felt like comfort wrapped in kindness. Those few moments before surgery always feel suspended in time; everything slows down, the air thick with anticipation.

Once the checks were done – name, date of birth, procedure – they wheeled me into theatre. The room was bright, almost too bright, and cold enough to make me shiver. I greeted the team, cracked a nervous joke, and felt the familiar sting of the anaesthetic moving through my veins. The world grew heavy and blurred, and I began my usual countdown – one, two, three, but didn't make it to four.

When I woke up, the pain hit hard. My abdomen throbbed and felt heavy. My eyelids were heavy too, too heavy to open, my mind foggy and slow. A nurse stayed beside me, her voice soft but steady, adjusting my pain relief until I felt more comfortable. Even through the haze, I registered her kindness. Small gestures matter when you feel at your most vulnerable.

After I had been moved from recovery to a private room, Mark was waiting, relief etched across his face. I've never liked the feeling of strong drugs in my system – that sense of being detached from myself, half-floating, half-fighting to stay present. I longed for clarity, to feel grounded in my own skin again. He stayed with me for a while, offering quiet companionship, but soon the medication pulled me into a deep, unavoidable sleep.

A laparoscopy, the procedure I had undergone, involves four small incisions across the abdomen – on the left and right, just below the bikini line, and at the belly button. The abnormal tissue growth in my body was cut out, a process called excision. My surgeon preferred this method over burning (ablation) because it reliably removes lesions, allows for confirmation through laboratory testing, and significantly reduces the risk of recurrence. Hours later, when I finally mustered the courage to look, I saw a drainage tube emerging from the left incision, connected to a bag slowly collecting the blood-tinged fluid from my abdomen. A catheter was in place and nurses administered regular injections in my thighs to prevent blood clots. I asked them to alternate legs because each jab left a deep, bruised ache. The gas used to expand my abdomen during surgery caused sharp pain that radiated up to my shoulders and lingered for days, until my body could gradually absorb it. Each incision was small, but each one felt monumental – battle scars, quiet proof of endurance.

The experience of surgery felt immense – a physically and emotionally demanding ordeal. A laparoscopy, performed by an endometriosis specialist, is the gold standard for diagnosis, assessing the extent of disease, and providing appropriate treatment. No scan, blood test, or non-invasive procedure can give a definitive answer, and there is no alternative way to remove the tissue or address damaged organs. Seeing a specialist is essential, as they have the expertise to identify and remove even subtle lesions that a general surgeon or non-specialist might miss. The reality is stark: you must go through something significant and invasive just to get certainty about what's happening inside your body.

The nurses were extraordinary – patient, unhurried, and deeply human. Even the unpleasant tasks, like removing the drainage tube the following day, were made bearable by their empathy. They explained each step, giving me something to hold onto – knowledge and agency, the sense that I still had choice and control – in a moment full of discomfort.

When the surgeon came to see me, I was still groggy but lucid enough to notice the weight of his expression. "You do have endometriosis," he said. "It's extremely severe – stage four. Your organs were fused together by endometrial tissue, so the surgery took longer than expected, more than three hours, but it went well."

He explained that nearly all the abnormal tissue had been removed, except for a small patch in a pocket behind my womb – the deepest part of the abdominal cavity and one of the hardest areas to reach. Then he showed me photos of my abdominal cavity. Photo after photo revealed what had been happening inside me all these years: adhesions stretching across nearly every organ and along my abdominal wall, and my organs fused together. The sheer scale was confronting and shocking. He paused, then asked, "How on earth did you put up with the pain for so long?"

How? Because I had no choice. When the world tells you your pain isn't real, you learn to carry it silently. You make it invisible so you can keep functioning. You keep showing up – for work, for friends, for family, and for life – even when your body begs you to stop.

The truth about endometriosis, however, is that surgery isn't a cure. There is no cure. Tissue removal brings relief, but often only temporarily. Mine lasted about seven months before the pain crept back – when I first felt the familiar ache, my heart sank. Fatigue set in, thick and relentless. My abdomen felt heavy again, as if packed with cement. And the nausea returned.

The operation cost over $5,000 (AUD), even with insurance – not to mention leave from work and study and the growing sense of dependence I despised. Almost two years later, the endometrioma had returned, leaving me to decide whether to keep the affected ovary or remove it. The knowledge that endometriomas carry a significant risk of ovarian cancer stayed with me, quietly shadowing every thought. Doctors can advise you, but they can't decide for you. In the end, you're the one who must live with the consequences.

I worried about how the surgery might affect me hormonally – ovaries produce oestrogen, progesterone, and small amounts of testosterone, all vital for fertility, bone strength, and muscle growth. Being in my early 40s, a time when these functions naturally start to decline, the decision carried extra weight. I felt like I was forcing my body to age faster than it should. But the alternative felt riskier. I trusted my instincts and agreed to another laparoscopy and a unilateral oophorectomy – the removal of one ovary.

Recovery from the second surgery felt endless. Even weeks later, I was reminded again and again to slow down. Exercise was out of the question. Focusing on what I couldn't do started to drag me into a dark place – frustration curdling into anger. I wanted my independence back and to feel like myself again. So, I started by breaking tasks into small, achievable steps. At first, it was replying to emails, paying bills – small markers of normal life. Then I set physical goals. Day one: make it outside the front door. Day two: the car. Day three: halfway down the driveway. They sound trivial, but they were everything – little declarations that I was still moving forward.

Focusing on progress, not limitation, became my lifeline. Over the next couple of weeks, I eased back into daily life and returned to work. Computer-based tasks were manageable, but the physical demands of farm work and everyday chores took far longer, requiring a slow, careful build. I was told by my surgeon to take it easy for at least six weeks. Still, my strength returned gradually, as I knew it would. I began to notice the quiet victories – standing a little longer, sitting a little straighter, breathing without pain.

Frustration still surfaced, but I learned to meet it with compassion. I'd already survived worse. This was another chapter, not the ending. I learned to give myself grace – accepting that my best would look different from day to day.

When the pain finally eased and I recovered from surgery, the relief was pure bliss. But as I'd come to learn, endometriosis has a cruel way of returning. In the months that followed, I began to understand that healing wasn't a finish line – it was a rhythm. Some days I moved forward with ease; others, I felt as if I was starting all over again. But somewhere within that repetition, I found strength in persistence itself. It wasn't about conquering pain but learning to live alongside it – to honour my body's limits without letting them define me.

For so long, I had equated resilience with pushing through, with grit and endurance. But recovery taught me a different version – one grounded in softness. It meant listening to my body when it wanted me to rest and not waiting until it screamed. It meant accepting help, even when pride resisted. And it meant learning that strength isn't measured by how much we endure, but by how we adapt.

Endometriosis changed my relationship with my body, but it also deepened my understanding of compassion – for myself, and for others carrying unseen pain with their own unique mental and physical health challenges. There's quiet courage in showing up for life, even when you're uncertain what the day will bring.

I no longer see my scars as reminders of what was broken, but as proof of what has healed – tangible evidence of survival, persistence, and grace. This chapter of my life wasn't the end of struggle, but the beginning of understanding what it truly means to live with resilience.

Lessons learned:

- **Healing is less about fixing my body and more about learning to live in partnership with it.** I've learned to see my body not as something broken, but as something to work with. Accepting what isn't in my control helps me use my energy wisely. Some days my body signals gently; other days it insists on rest – either way, paying attention allows me to move through life with greater ease and less resistance.

- **Listening to my body, even when it feels inconvenient, helps me make better decisions.** I can choose to push through pain and ignore early warning signs; however, tuning in early helps prevent bigger setbacks. Checking in with myself – noticing fatigue, tension, or subtle changes – guides when to rest and when to lean in. Listening is an act of respect, not weakness.

- **Researching my condition helps me stay informed and reduces uncertainty.** Understanding my condition gives me a voice in my own care. Reading, asking questions, and creating simple notes or visual summaries helps me remember information and feel more confident. Knowledge doesn't take away the difficulty, but it gives me direction and a sense of control in unpredictable times.

- **Focusing on what I *can* do helps me stay positive and grounded.** Chronic illness can make your world feel small, but even small achievements matter. On tough days, I focus on what's within reach – small tasks, moments of calm, or gentle movement. Celebrating what I *can* do keeps me hopeful and reminds me that progress exists in many forms.

- **My best looks different on different days – and that's okay.** Some days I can give a lot; other days I can barely manage the basics. Both are valid. Letting go of the need to always perform has brought a sense of freedom. My worth isn't measured by productivity – it's measured by how I care for myself through it all.

- **Acceptance doesn't mean giving up – it means choosing peace where I can.** There's power in acknowledging what's outside my control. When I stop fighting reality, I make space for calm and clarity. Acceptance lets me focus on what I *can* influence, creating space for peace instead of constant struggle.

PART TWO:

BENEATH THE SKIN

THREE

SCIENCE BEHIND THE SYMPTOMS

OUR BODIES ARE INTRICATE SYSTEMS in which every function is interconnected – no symptom exists in isolation. Fatigue, nausea, and pain often overlap, feeding into one another through shared biological pathways. When the body experiences ongoing stress, inflammation, or hormonal changes, these symptoms can be amplified in a cycle that affects both physical and emotional wellbeing. Researching my condition to help understand this connection helps explain why some days feel so overwhelming – and offers insight into how I can begin to break that cycle and restore balance.

Fatigue: when rest isn't enough

Fatigue in endometriosis is not simply a matter of poor sleep or low motivation – it's a deep physiological exhaustion. Even after long hours of rest, my body feels fatigued, as though it never had a chance to recover. This isn't imagined; it's the result of complex biological processes that keep my body in a constant state of alert.

Endometriosis is recognised as a systemic inflammatory condition, not just a disorder confined to the pelvis. Lesions release inflammatory molecules called cytokines, which activate the immune system and influence how the brain regulates energy and alertness. These same chemical messengers are behind the deep, flu-like fatigue that people with endometriosis often experience – the immune system is constantly "on", even when the body should be resting.

Hormones play a crucial role as well. Many people with endometriosis experience oestrogen dominance and low progesterone, a combination that can disrupt sleep cycles, heighten stress hormones, and reduce restorative deep sleep. Pain adds another layer, keeping the nervous system in a state of hyperarousal – often described as "wired but tired". Over time, this chronic activation can deplete energy reserves and blunt the body's ability to repair itself.

Research has also shown that the tiny structures inside cells responsible for producing energy don't work as efficiently in endometrial tissue. When the body struggles to generate enough energy to fuel basic cellular functions, fatigue becomes almost unavoidable. Add to this the nutrient losses that often come with menstrual bleeding or gut inflammation, and energy levels can drop sharply.

Fatigue in endometriosis is real, measurable, and multi-layered. It is not a sign of weakness, laziness, or lack of effort – it's a reflection of a body working tirelessly beneath the surface. Understanding the biological roots of this exhaustion has helped me replace frustration with compassion, allowing me to approach my fatigue with both science and self-kindness. Years ago, I would beat myself up with endless "I should" statements whenever I wasn't at my best, only deepening the frustration. Over time, as I learned more about the condition, I consciously tried to honour my body for all that it endures rather than berate it for what it cannot do. I strive, and continue to strive, to be in awe of my body, recognising its resilience even on the hardest days.

Nausea: the relentless undercurrent

Nausea is one of the most overlooked yet debilitating symptoms of endometriosis. For me, it's persistent, often intensifying during flare-ups (a sudden surge of intense pelvic pain and fatigue, sometimes accompanied by bloating that last for days). While it is easy to dismiss nausea as a secondary symptom, science shows it is a direct consequence of how endometriosis affects the body's inflammatory, hormonal, and nervous systems.

Chronic inflammation lies at the core. The lesions that release chemical messengers – prostaglandins, cytokines, and other inflammatory molecules – trigger inflammation and sensitise local nerves. These signals also affect the autonomic nervous system and gut–brain pathways, including the vagus nerve, which connects to brain centres that control nausea. This helps explain why pelvic pain is often accompanied by queasiness, cramping, and digestive discomfort.

Managing nausea is a constant battle – nausea is an unrelenting presence that steals my appetite, disrupts hydration, and slowly dulls my zest for life. There've been countless moments where I've had to force myself to eat, not because I wanted to, but because I know the consequences of not eating are far worse. I've learned to keep things simple: basic, nourishing meals like chicken, brown rice, and vegetables. It's not exciting, but it's gentle fuel that keeps my body going without provoking further chaos.

Pain: the hallmark of endometriosis

Pain is more than a symptom –- it becomes a way of life. It's not the intensity alone that wears me down, but the persistence, the way it endures and refuses to let go. The constant, lingering ache, day and night, and the sharp, intense pain that strikes without warning and fades just as quickly. It can feel as though every organ is being crushed and twisted in a tight vice. But the pain isn't just confined to my pelvis; I feel it across my back and down my legs to my knees too. And it all stems from complex biological mechanisms that extend far beyond the reproductive system.

Endometriosis pain starts with inflammation, as prostaglandins and cytokines sensitise nearby nerves. Over time, these nerves become hyper-responsive, sending pain signals to the brain even when the initial trigger is minor or absent – a process known as peripheral sensitisation. If this cycle persists, chronic pain can reshape the brain itself through central sensitisation. When the nervous system is bombarded with pain signals for months or years, the brain's pain-processing centres become overactive and less able to 'turn off' the alarm. In practical terms, this means the nervous system can generate pain even in the absence of ongoing tissue damage, creating a self-sustaining echo that lingers long after the original trigger.

Hormonal fluctuations can play a key role in pain sensitivity in endometriosis. Oestrogen can encourage nerve growth within endometrial lesions, amplifying the tissue's response to inflammatory signals. In contrast, progesterone and progestin-based therapies appear to have a modulatory effect: when present, they may help limit nerve growth and dampen inflammatory signalling. Reduced or ineffective progesterone signalling, however, could weaken this modulatory influence, potentially allowing nerves to proliferate and pain sensitivity to increase. Adding to the complexity, overlapping nerve pathways connecting the gut, pelvis, and lower back can cause pain to spread or radiate in unpredictable ways.

Constant pain is not a sign of weakness; it is a reflection of neurological rewiring and immune overactivation. The body learns pain as a habit – and unlearning it requires a multifaceted approach. When I understand the biology of chronic pain, my perspective changes from self-blame to self-compassion. This is my body's way of protecting me, and now I can support its recovery.

One of the simplest yet most effective tools I've found for managing endometriosis pain is heat therapy. My heat belt has become a constant companion – not just for comfort, but for its science-backed benefits. Applying gentle, sustained warmth to the abdomen helps relax pelvic muscles, increase blood flow, and ease cramping caused by prostaglandin-driven contractions. The heat also activates thermoreceptors in the skin, sending competing signals to the brain that reduce pain perception – a mechanism known as the gate control theory of pain.

Beyond the biology, there's a deep psychological comfort in warmth. It communicates safety to the nervous system, helping shift the body out of fight-or-flight mode into a state of calm and rest. Using my heat belt has become a regular ritual – a grounding act of care that reminds me I can support my body, even on the hardest days. One of the things I love most is its practicality: it wraps easily around my waist with Velcro, fits discreetly under clothes, and has two rechargeable battery packs – so while one's in use, the other is charging and ready to go.

Over time, I've also learned to be mindful about relying on painkillers. While they can offer short-term relief, frequent use can sometimes disrupt the body's natural pain-regulation systems. Non-steroidal anti-inflammatory drugs, for example, work by blocking prostaglandins – the same inflammatory chemicals involved in endometriosis pain – but as I understand, long-term or excessive use can irritate the stomach lining, affect kidney function, and even lead to "rebound pain" as the body compensates for the suppression of inflammation. Opioid medications pose additional risks, as they can alter the brain's reward and pain circuits, reducing natural endorphin production and increasing sensitivity to pain over time – a phenomenon known as opioid-induced hyperalgesia. Whenever possible, I manage pain through movement, mindfulness, and heat therapy – approaches that support my body's resilience rather than silence its signals. I reserve pain medication for when the pain becomes truly disruptive, the kind that pulls me away from work or robs me of sleep – usually around a five out of ten on the pain scale.

Flare-ups: the unpredictable storm

Flare-ups are one of the most unpredictable and challenging aspects of living with endometriosis, and for me, one of the hardest to navigate. Scientifically, flare-ups occur when a combination of hormonal fluctuations, immune system activation, and inflammatory responses converge. The release of prostaglandins and cytokines – the same inflammatory molecules that influence fatigue, nausea, and pain – irritate the surrounding tissues and nerves. Hormonal changes too – particularly spikes or drops in oestrogen and progesterone throughout the menstrual cycle – can amplify this inflammatory response, making pain more intense. Stress, diet, and even subtle changes in gut health can further trigger or worsen flare-ups, creating a cascade effect that spreads beyond the pelvis. Because these triggers are unpredictable, flare-ups feel like an invisible minefield: one moment I'm managing, the next I'm struck by pain, fatigue, and nausea. Understanding biology helps me rationalise the chaos, but it doesn't make the experience any less exhausting or predictable.

What I find hardest about flare-ups is their unpredictability – you never know when one will show up. They've arrived at the most inconvenient moments: weekends away, birthdays, dinner with friends, overseas holidays, graduations – all the occasions I've looked forward to. In a split second, everything can change. I push through, determined to enjoy the moment as best I can, but whether I like it or not, my mood and enjoyment level take a hit. That's when my "brave face" goes into full effect – I'm outwardly calm and composed, while inside I'm desperate for relief.

Digestion: the importance of gut health

Diet plays a crucial role in managing endometriosis because the condition is deeply linked to inflammation, hormonal balance, and immune function. Certain foods can either exacerbate or help reduce chronic inflammation – a key driver of endometriosis pain. Diets high in saturated fats, red meat, and processed foods have been associated with increased prostaglandin production, which can intensify pain and trigger inflammatory responses. Conversely, anti-inflammatory foods such as leafy greens, fatty fish rich in omega-3s, and high-fibre fruits and vegetables can help modulate immune activity, regulate oestrogen levels, and support the body's natural detoxification pathways.

Maintaining stable blood sugar by prioritising complex carbohydrates and limiting highly processed sugars can help reduce systemic inflammation and hormonal fluctuations. Research shows that high-glycaemic diets and sugar spikes can worsen inflammation, increase oxidative stress, and heighten pain sensitivity, all of which can make endometriosis symptoms harder to manage. Hormonal fluctuations add another layer of complexity: around menstruation, sharp drops in oestrogen and progesterone can alter gut motility and stomach acid balance, further influencing digestive comfort and symptom severity. Oestrogen also influences the production of serotonin – much of which is made in the gut – and when levels swing, digestion and appetite regulation can be disrupted. Pain medications and slower digestion can further contribute, and many people with endometriosis experience gut hypersensitivity or mild dysbiosis (an imbalance in the gut microbiome), sometimes called "endo belly". Endo belly can make the abdomen look swollen or distended, sometimes unevenly, resembling pregnancy or severe bloating, with the stomach feeling tight, hard, or tender to the touch. It can be especially frustrating in the warmer months when hoodies and baggy clothes aren't an option. With my tiny frame, endo belly can be obvious, but I've learned to accept it for what it is – sometimes even having a chuckle about it. It's either that or let it get the better of me, and I refuse to give it that power.

Lifestyle: finding balance in chaos

While lifestyle adjustments alone cannot cure endometriosis, scientific evidence strongly supports the idea that combining an anti-inflammatory diet, regular physical activity, and stress management strategies can significantly improve symptom management, reduce flare-ups, and enhance overall wellbeing. Taking a holistic approach helps me work with my body, giving me a stronger sense of control over my health.

For me, physical activity is a critical component and something I adopt in my everyday life. Regular movement – including cardiovascular exercise, strength training, and flexibility work – helps improve circulation, reduce inflammatory markers, and balance hormone levels. Exercise has been shown to increase endorphins, the body's natural painkillers, and enhance mood, which is particularly important given the link between chronic pain, stress, and mental health. Yoga, Pilates, or gentle stretching can also support pelvic floor function, relieve tension, and reduce painful flare-ups. I strive to move every day – exercise nourishes not just my body, but also my mind. No matter how I feel beforehand, I've never regretted it afterward.

Getting adequate sleep, managing stress, and maintaining a consistent routine amplify these benefits. Poor sleep or chronic stress can increase cortisol, a stress hormone, which can disrupt immune function, exacerbate inflammation, and worsen pain. Mind–body practices such as deep breathing and mindfulness help me regulate the stress response, supporting my hormonal and immune systems in parallel with diet and exercise.

Comorbidities: the layers of living with endometriosis

Endometriosis is often thought of as a condition confined to the reproductive system, but research increasingly shows it can affect the body more broadly. One reason for this is the concept of comorbidities – medical conditions that coexist alongside a primary diagnosis. In the case of endometriosis, comorbidities are not simply coincidental; they often share underlying mechanisms such as chronic inflammation, immune dysregulation, or hormonal imbalances. Recognising these links is crucial because it allows me to take a more proactive approach to my overall health.

Several studies have highlighted conditions that are more common in people with endometriosis. For example, autoimmune disorders such as thyroid disease, lupus, and rheumatoid arthritis appear at higher rates, suggesting that the immune system in those with endometriosis may be hyperactive or misdirected. Cardiovascular risk is also elevated, potentially due to systemic inflammation and lifestyle impacts of chronic pain. Additionally, bone health can be affected; research suggests that hormonal imbalances, especially low progesterone and long-term use of certain hormonal therapies, may increase the risk of osteoporosis over time.

Other linked conditions include gastrointestinal disorders like irritable bowel syndrome, migraines, and mental health conditions such as anxiety and depression, which are often exacerbated by chronic pain and fatigue. These comorbidities underscore the importance of viewing endometriosis as a systemic condition, rather than isolating it to the pelvis. Awareness of potential comorbidities allows for earlier interventions – whether through lifestyle modifications, monitoring, or collaboration with specialists – and ultimately helps improve quality of life.

By understanding the broader health landscape surrounding endometriosis, I can advocate for comprehensive care that addresses both symptoms and associated risks, rather than simply managing pain or menstrual irregularities in isolation.

FOUR

MIND–BODY CONNECTION

CONTEMPORARY NEUROSCIENCE SHOWS THAT THE mind and body are not separate systems but interconnected networks in constant, dynamic exchange. Pain is not simply a signal of tissue damage; it is an experience shaped by the brain's interpretation of threat, emotion, and past experience. For years, I understood my symptoms purely in physical terms – inflammation, hormones, flare-ups. But over time, I realised that my emotional state, stress levels, and even self-beliefs played just as powerful a role. The more I understood the mind–body interaction, the clearer it became that managing pain isn't about suppressing it with positive thinking, but about interpreting the complex messages shared between the brain and body.

I am the sum of my thoughts: the mind–body dialogue

Mindfulness, self-compassion, and reflective practices have been central to understanding my mind–body dialogue. I've learned to pause and acknowledge sensations without immediately labelling them as "bad" or "weakness", instead reframing my experiences with curiosity rather than criticism. Over time, these practices have helped me break cycles of catastrophic thinking, reduce anticipatory anxiety, and reclaim a sense of agency.

Psychological resilience isn't about ignoring pain – it's about responding to it adaptively. Cognitive restructuring involves recognising unhelpful thoughts and reframing them. Long before I studied psychology, I practised this instinctively, shifting *I can't do this, it's all too hard* to *I can do this. I am strong. I've done it before, and I'll do it again.* Over the years, that simple shift became a skill I applied to everything – pacing work tasks, navigating flare-ups, completing uni assignments, and running ultramarathons.

Unhelpful thinking could easily have derailed me – eroding my confidence, isolating me from others, and straining relationships. Cognitive reframing, along with boundary-setting, became essential. These skills allow me to live in ways that respect both my limits and my potential, minimising mental and emotional exhaustion. But they haven't come easily. Boundary-setting has always been difficult – a lesson learned through experience. Deciding when to rest, when to seek medical attention, and when to push through requires reflective thinking, emotional regulation, and self-trust. Each decision is filtered through cognitive patterns shaped by past trauma, societal expectations, and internalised messages about strength and endurance. Recognising those mental patterns has allowed me to respond more intentionally, rather than automatically.

For years, I pushed myself to please others, even when I was struggling. Saying no or expressing my needs felt selfish. Now, it's a constant balancing act – learning to recognise when giving too much of myself comes at the expense of my wellbeing and understanding that saying no is not selfish, but an act of self-respect. The psychology behind it is complex – ingrained habits, fear of disappointing others, and a desire for control make boundaries difficult to maintain, even when my body demands them. I've realised that boundaries don't just protect my body – they safeguard the things that truly matter: my energy, my wellbeing, and my peace of mind.

Learning to check in with myself became second nature – a monumental skill that later proved invaluable in endurance events like ultramarathons. After years of having my pain dismissed by the medical profession, rebuilding trust in my body was a slow process. I had to relearn that pain doesn't always mean harm; sometimes it's simply heightened sensitivity shaped by years of distress. By cultivating self-awareness, I began interpreting my body's signals differently – not as threats, but as information. When discomfort arises, I pause and ask, *What is my body trying to tell me right now?* That small shift – toward curiosity – changes everything. It's not about controlling pain, but about rebuilding partnership with my body, one grounded in compassion rather than mistrust.

Just as I've learned to listen more compassionately to my own body, I've also had to learn how to filter the noise of the outside world. In an age where comparison is constant, social media can make body image and chronic illness even harder to navigate. Everywhere I look, I see young, toned, flawless bodies – curated snapshots of perfection that rarely show the full story. It's all too easy to fall into the trap of comparison, measuring myself against filtered ideals and feeling inadequate. But those moments are reminders to pause and recalibrate. The bodies we see online capture a single, edited moment – not the complexity of real life. My body has carried me through surgeries, flare-ups, exhaustion, and recovery. It deserves compassion, not criticism. Shifting my focus from appearance to appreciation has been part of redefining strength – seeing beauty not in perfection, but in values like kindness, honesty, and integrity.

It's not all bad, though. When used with intention, social media can be an incredible source of connection and motivation. I love sharing laughs with friends, sending funny reels, or drawing inspiration from people whose courage and resilience move me. Turia Pitt, an Australian ultramarathon runner who survived catastrophic burns to 65% of her body after being caught in a bushfire during an event in the Kimberley Region, Western Australia, and Nedd Brockmann, who ran 4,000 kilometres across Australia to raise money for homelessness, are two that truly stand out. Despite immense challenges, they continue to show up – for themselves and for others. Their strength reminds me that true beauty runs far deeper than what's visible; it lives in perseverance, kindness, and purpose.

But while stories like theirs inspire me, they also highlight how rare it is to see such authenticity reflected in everyday life. Most of the time, our thoughts don't exist in isolation – they're shaped by the values and expectations we absorb from family, peers, school, and the culture around us. As a society, we prioritise achievement, productivity, appearance, and control – often over vulnerability or rest. From a young age, many of us are taught to "be strong", "look perfect", and "keep it together", yet rarely given tools to process emotions or handle setbacks. This cultural framework fuels perfectionism, comparison, and self-criticism – the roots of anxiety, depression, and disconnection from the body's signals. And its effects start early. It saddens me to see young girls told to suppress pain or push through discomfort, internalising the message that their needs are inconvenient. They learn to distrust their bodies, as I once did: *I shouldn't feel this way. I must be weak.* But these thought patterns don't stay in the mind – they shape the body. Stress hormones surge, muscles tense, digestion slows, and pain intensifies. The body reacts to the mind, and the mind reacts to the body, creating a loop of suffering that's hard to break.

With social media amplifying these pressures, the impact has become profound. The constant exposure to "perfect" lives fosters unrealistic standards and deepens self-doubt. Young people, especially girls, internalise these ideals before they've fully developed a sense of self. The result is a generation increasingly disconnected from their bodies, battling anxiety, low self-worth, and chronic stress. These mental struggles often manifest physically – just as mine did – and, too often, they're dismissed.

Challenging these societal narratives and rebuilding trust in the body isn't just self-work – it's resistance. Relearning that my sensations, emotions, and pain are valid signals – not failures – has been transformative. It's a lesson I wish was taught young: that strength isn't about ignoring the body, hiding pain, or striving for perfection. True strength lies in listening, understanding, and responding with care – mentally, emotionally, and physically.

The pain loop: how the body and brain interact

In endometriosis, real and measurable biological processes drive the pain; inflammation, hormonal changes, and nerve hypersensitivity create a constant storm of physical signals. Over time, though, the brain learns to interpret these ongoing messages as signs of danger.

I'm not imagining the pain – my brain is amplifying it in an attempt to protect me. Every twinge, every wave of discomfort, becomes magnified by a nervous system on high alert.

The result is a complex feedback loop between body and brain. The pain is real, but so is the brain's learned anticipation of it. Living with this means pain is never purely physical; it's also emotional, cognitive, and social. The constant pain signals shape my attention, mood, and even memory, turning daily life into a balancing act between endurance and adaptation.

Early on, when I learned to internalise pain – breaking time into fragments just to get through the day – I wasn't simply using endurance tactics; I was employing an instinctive form of self-regulation. My brain was managing attention, emotion, and energy under unrelenting stress. My body was surviving, and my mind was doing its best to keep up.

Because the brain is naturally wired to detect potential threats – a survival mechanism – a body in constant distress can keep the mind on high alert. When my body continuously sends pain signals, my brain becomes hyperfocused on them. This vigilance intensifies the experience of pain while draining mental energy, reinforcing the feeling that life itself is exhausting.

Trauma adds another layer to this mind–body dialogue. When pain is repeatedly dismissed or minimised – especially by medical professionals – it doesn't just hurt emotionally; it reshapes the nervous system. Each invalidating encounter reinforces the message that my body can't be trusted, that its signals are wrong or exaggerated. Over time, this erodes self-trust and creates what psychologists call hypervigilance: a constant scanning for danger, both physical and emotional. My body became a site of uncertainty – a place I lived in but didn't always feel safe inhabiting. Even after I finally received a diagnosis, that pattern of vigilance lingered, like a reflex I couldn't fully unlearn.

Chronic pain also alters the brain's reward and motivation systems. When everything is exhausting, even small wins feel monumental. I learned to celebrate completing tasks that others might take for granted – like making it through a commute or finishing a work project despite fatigue. Psychologically, these moments of mastery help recalibrate the brain's reward pathways, counteracting the demoralisation that chronic illness can bring. This mindset became invaluable later in life, particularly when running ultramarathons, where endurance is as much psychological as physical.

Another crucial concept is interoception – the brain's ability to sense internal bodily signals. In endometriosis, inflammation, hormonal fluctuations, and pain disrupt this communication, making the body feel unpredictable or unreliable. My brain learned to anticipate discomfort, which created anticipatory anxiety. This isn't imagined; it's the result of adaptive neuroplasticity – a body–brain system working to survive chronic stress. Learning to notice these anticipatory thoughts, without letting them take over, has become a daily practice in mindfulness and self-compassion.

Stress hormones further complicate this dynamic. Cortisol, released during chronic stress, amplifies both inflammation and pain perception. Psychologically, this shows up as irritability, anxiety, and difficulty concentrating, creating a self-reinforcing feedback loop: stress worsens symptoms, and worsening symptoms increase stress. Understanding this cycle shifted my perspective – coping wasn't about sheer willpower; it was about recognising how closely intertwined physiological and psychological factors are. I realised that much of my stress came from everyday life, not just major events. Long commutes to work meant hours away from home, high-pressure work left me drained, and by the time I got a moment to myself, I was too exhausted or pressed for time to engage in activities that truly nourished me – paddleboarding, running, or spending time with my horses. This combination of small, repeated stressors kept the loop running on autopilot, until I reminded myself that I was in control and could choose to reclaim my time, energy, and wellbeing.

Ultimately, understanding the mind–body dialogue has transformed how I experience chronic illness. Pain is no longer simply a signal to endure or suppress; it is a message, a form of communication from a body and brain striving to survive, adapt, and protect. Learning to interpret these messages with curiosity and compassion – rather than fear or frustration – has allowed me to reclaim agency in a life shaped by endometriosis. It's a practice that encompasses more than just managing symptoms: it involves rebuilding trust in myself, setting boundaries that honour my needs, and challenging societal pressures that tell us to ignore discomfort or prioritise appearance over wellbeing. Mindfulness, cognitive reframing, and reflective practices are not just coping strategies – they are tools for empowerment, enabling me to navigate flare-ups, fatigue, and uncertainty with intention. Recognising that my thoughts, emotions, and bodily sensations are interconnected has also highlighted the importance of resisting cultural messages that undermine self-trust – messages that teach young girls to ignore their instincts, push through pain for the sake of appearance or achievement, and measure their worth against curated images of perfection. In embracing this holistic perspective, I've come to see resilience not as heroic endurance or the absence of pain, but as the ongoing, conscious dialogue between mind and body – a dialogue that transforms suffering into insight, frustration into understanding, and limitation into possibility.

Practical takeaways:

- **Acknowledge my thoughts**. Chronic pain and fatigue often come with a flood of automatic, unhelpful thoughts: *I can't do this* or *I'm weak*. I simply pause and observe them. Acknowledging the thought and reflecting can reduce its power and helps me respond more intentionally.

- **Practise cognitive reframing**. Once I've noticed an unhelpful thought, I consciously shift it to a more balanced perspective: *I can do this in small steps*. Over time, this has retrained my brain to reduce unhelpful catastrophic thinking.

- **Tune in to my body signals**. Instead of ignoring fatigue, pain, or flare-ups, I pause and reflect on what my body might be telling me. I ask myself: *Do I need rest? Movement? Medical attention?* Listening reduces stress and helps prevent symptom escalation.

- **Set boundaries and protect my energy**. Psychologically, it's essential I recognise my limits. Saying no, delegating, or rescheduling tasks is not weakness – it's self-preservation. Boundaries protect mental and physical energy, reducing stress in my mind and body.

- **Practise mindfulness and self-compassion.** Mindfulness allows me to observe sensations without judgement, while self-compassion teaches me to treat myself as I would a loved one. Together, these practices help break cycles of guilt, shame, and frustration.

- **Seek support when needed.** I surround myself with trusted friends who are genuine, considerate, and have a good sense of humour. Sometimes, being able to laugh together is just as important as talking through the hard stuff.

- **Remember that comparison is a waste of energy.** My body, my challenges, my victories – they cannot be measured against anyone else's.

PART THREE:

ROOTS OF RESILIENCE

FIVE

THE ARCHITECTURE OF CHILDHOOD

CHILDHOOD IS LIKE A MOSAIC slowly taking shape – each memory a small, imperfect piece. At the time, you don't always see the colours or how the fragments fit together; some are bright and joyful, others dark and jagged. For me, only with distance does the image begin to make sense, revealing patterns that shaped who I became and the resilience I would later draw upon.

I grew up in a low socioeconomic household, where financial stress was a quiet, constant presence. As a child, it was simply life. Bills stacked up, outings were rare, and treats were luxuries rather than expectations. I didn't notice the strain then – I accepted it as normal – but as I grew older, I began to sense the contrast between my world and that of others. I never resented my parents or my circumstances – they simply shaped me in ways I would only understand later. Living with constraints taught me creativity, patience, and an appreciation for small joys that others might take for granted.

I was a shy child who disliked being the centre of attention, though around familiar faces I'd come out of my shell – much as I do now. Some of my fondest memories are from the 80s, playing with the neighbourhood kids. There were six of us – my sister Alana and I, and two sets of siblings from the neighbourhood – all around the same age. We'd drift between each other's houses, stopping for cordial or chips between trampoline turns, before settling on the curb or in someone's backyard with ice-cold Sunnyboys, the summer heat softened by the shade of a tree. As long as we were home by dinner, we could roam free all day. There were no phones or screens – just the quiet signal of friendship: a pile of bikes laid on a front lawn. That freedom felt boundless. Even in retrospect, I can still hear the laughter echoing in the street, the squeak of trampoline springs, and the clicking sound of the Spokey Dokeys on my bike wheels.

At age four, I told Dad I wanted to be a singing nurse. Even now, that combination makes me smile – but in hindsight, it makes perfect sense. I had a deep desire to help others heal. While the job never existed, and I'm pretty sure it still doesn't, the impulse – to nurture, comfort, and mend – followed me throughout my life. It wasn't just about treating illness; even then, I wanted to restore joy and balance, to bring calm in moments of chaos. That instinct to care, to understand, and to comfort has become a throughline in my adult life, manifesting in both my academic pursuits and my professional choices.

Music has always been part of that. It carried me through pain, loss, and transition, shaping my emotions in ways I couldn't understand as a child. My earliest memories of music are intertwined with movement and play – singing to cassettes or the radio, dancing to songs in the living room, or listening to CDs in my room, alone. Music provided a private sanctuary, a place to feel without judgement. Now, as a psychology student, I can see what that early dream represented: both music and psychology are forms of healing – one through rhythm and emotion, the other through understanding and connection. Even as a little girl, I was unknowingly searching for ways to bring both together, to restore balance in myself and others.

When I was growing up, my parents shaped my world in very different ways, their contrasting personalities leaving a lasting imprint on who I am today. Dad was born in England in 1931 and grew up under the shadow of World War II. He lived through air raids, rationing, and evacuation programs, experiences he rarely spoke of – but I remember the small box he kept, filled with shrapnel, tangible echoes of a childhood shaped by conflict. He began work delivering newspapers before developing an interest in carpentry, taking a position at a hat block maker's workshop where he handled a variety of tasks – building tables and stools, cleaning machinery, and running errands. At age 20, he joined the Royal Air Force, which acted as a training ground where he could gain exposure to mechanical, electrical, and logistical skills – preparing him for trades that were in high demand in post-war Britain. Eight years later, at 28, he migrated to Australia with his first wife. After that relationship ended, he married Mum in 1972 and settled into life as a painter and decorator – a profession that would shape much of my childhood.

I used to go with him to jobs, proudly wielding a scraper or brush – peeling wallpaper, masking edges, sanding. Even in primary school, I loved feeling included, being part of the rhythm of his craft. He had a natural warmth and easy rapport with clients, and I suspect he let me handle the small prep tasks just to keep me occupied – otherwise, I'd be chatting away, making it hard for him to focus. Those days weren't just about painting walls – they were about being together. Sharing the work, side by side, I learned lessons in patience, attention to detail, and quiet pride. Watching him move through each task, I understood how even the simplest jobs could carry a sense of dignity, and how meaningful it was to simply be part of his world.

Dad brought laughter into my life and radiated warmth and calm. He nurtured my curiosity and awe for the world, filling our home with stories, jokes, and laughter that drew others in at every gathering. He was a reflective person – something I now recognise as invaluable, especially as a psychology student, given how reflection shapes understanding of self and others. Every evening, he'd write in his diary, documenting both the monumental and the ordinary moments of life. As a child, I never questioned it – I simply assumed it was part of his nightly routine, something that had woven itself into his life so naturally it seemed second nature. Alana now keeps all his diaries at her house, offering glimpses into his thoughts and the life he quietly chronicled – a treasure trove of reflection and memory.

Just as his diaries captured the quiet rhythms of his life, the pages of his National Geographic magazines opened windows to the wider world, fuelling my own curiosity and sense of wonder from a young age. I would pull them off the shelf and spend hours flipping through pages of unfamiliar landscapes, animals, and cultures. I had no understanding of the context, yet the images moved me deeply, eliciting feelings of wonder, empathy, and connection. That love of photography – of capturing emotion and sharing it – remains with me today, as it did with Dad.

Mum, in her own way, shaped me too. Born in 1948, she grew up in Melbourne and pursued a career in accounting. Throughout my childhood, she worked in various accounting roles, and her sharp wit and sociable nature shone through. She loved engaging in conversation, enjoyed dinners and theatre outings with friends, and spent the occasional weekend at pubs listening to live music. But she also carried challenges that I couldn't understand as a child – and perhaps never fully will. I remember her nervous breakdown when I was eight. Moments of closeness were interspersed with times of withdrawal. Those early experiences quietly taught me to self-soothe, manage stress, and intuitively gauge when to step back and when to engage – lessons that became the foundation of my emotional resilience.

Understanding my early life also means recognising the trauma that preceded it. Mum lost her father in a car accident when I was four months old. He was killed by a drunk driver. I can only imagine the shock, grief, and altered worldview that loss created. I often wonder how her experience of profound grief affected her capacity to connect with me – and, in turn, how it shaped my attachment patterns. Years later, studying psychology, attachment theory gave words to what I had lived. Early connection – or its absence – with caregivers shapes emotional regulation, perception of safety, and trust. I was particularly struck by the Still Face Experiment – a study in which a mother first engages playfully with her baby, mirroring expressions and cooing in tune with her child's emotions. Then she suddenly becomes expressionless and unresponsive. Within seconds, the infant's demeanour shifts from curiosity to confusion, then distress, desperately trying to draw her mother's attention back through smiles, gestures, and cries. When the mother finally re-engages, the baby's relief is palpable – a mix of joy and lingering uncertainty. It's a powerful demonstration of how deeply we rely, even as infants, on emotional attunement and safety. Watching it, I recognised my own early experiences: the tension of reaching for comfort and finding absence, and the subtle ways such disconnection can ripple across a lifetime. I can never be sure what our relationship was like during my infant years, but this experiment always makes me wonder.

Through it all, I was shaped as much by disconnection as by connection. Research on early adversity shows that children from changing environments often develop hypervigilance, problem-solving skills, and subtle coping mechanisms that go unnoticed. In my case, these traits manifested as quiet observation, emotional self-sufficiency, and an unwavering determination to keep going, even when circumstances felt overwhelming.

Adolescence brought its own challenges. My parents divorced when I was a teenager. Alana, who is four years older than me, moved in with Dad, and I stayed with Mum. Alana was someone I looked up to throughout childhood. Naturally, I copied much of what she did, which I know completely frustrated her. She was the benchmark against which I measured myself, and in many ways, she modelled confidence that I admired. Up until my parents' divorce, we had a typical sibling relationship; you know the one – best friends one minute, fighting the next. But as she started to approach adulthood, I could see a whole new world had opened for her to explore – and, rightly, she did. After we stopped living together as a family, our shared time gradually became less frequent. I began to find my own ways of navigating the world, learning to make decisions independently, solving problems on my own, and relying on my instincts. Those early experiences, though challenging, quietly built resilience, teaching me that I could adapt even when the familiar support around me shifted.

It was tense between Mum and me when we were living together – full of arguments, silences, and the constant negotiation of independence. In an old journal from when I was 17, I wrote, "*I feel like I don't belong anywhere.*" Reading those words decades later filled me with sadness. Mum was absorbed in her own world, Alana exploring her newfound freedom, and Dad navigating the aftermath of divorce. I longed to reach back and hug that young girl – to offer her the compassion and reassurance she hadn't yet learned to give herself.

Admittedly, I lost my way as a teenager. The freedom I experienced in my late teens might have seemed like a dream for some, but for me, it began to lead in directions I knew were undesirable. I was surrounded by smoking, drinking, and drug use – behaviours that were abundant in my social circles, making the opportunities all too easy to come by.

I often recall an early psychology assignment on nature versus nurture – exploring how our biology and environment shape who we are and the choices we make. My environment exposed me to risk, and yet, left largely to my own devices, I made choices that kept me away from hard drugs and excessive drinking. Despite feeling lost, frustrated, and unbound by structure, I somehow navigated those pressures without succumbing.

Looking back, I think a lot of it came down to my personality traits – perhaps a tendency toward conscientiousness, self-regulation, and internalised values. Developmental psychology suggests that even in risky environments, certain protective factors – like innate temperament, early life experiences, or cognitive reflection – can influence decision-making. For me, those factors quietly guided my choices, even when my external world felt chaotic.

That inner steadiness became even more important within our small family in Australia – just my mum's side: my cousin Tahlia, my aunty Leanne, and my nanna – because in such a small unit, every emotion, every shift, and every challenge felt amplified. Having something solid and calm inside myself helped me navigate it all. Tahlia is six months older than me, and she admired my sister just as much as I did. So when the three of us played together, I, as the youngest, almost always ended up being "it" in our games of tiggy. I was often the one running, dodging, or getting squished playing corners in the car. Despite the teasing, we spent a lot of time together, especially during holidays, and had so much fun.

My nanna passed away when I was 16, and over the years my connection with Leanne and Tahlia faded. In contrast, my family in the UK was much larger, and I have fond memories of relatives visiting. We did all the touristy things, shared family dinners, and spent hours being entertained by their stories and antics. Those moments left me with some of my happiest childhood memories – and shaped much of the environment in which I grew up, including the values, routines, and interests that surrounded me.

Although my early world was full of imagination, stories, and exploration, organised sport was never a central part of our family life. Movement was part of play – riding bikes, running through the street with friends, jumping on trampolines – but structured sport was something different altogether. I tried Little Athletics at the age of six and joined cross-country in primary school, even reaching state level, but by high school, PE was my least favourite subject – alongside History. I wasn't naturally athletic, and my family didn't prioritise movement. Dad did enjoy watching cricket in summer, often with playful rivalry against our UK relatives during the Australia vs England Ashes series, but we were never encouraged to play sport outside of school. Feeling unskilled, I never imagined pursuing it seriously. It would only be later that I discovered how deeply physical activity could contribute to my wellbeing, resilience, and self-efficacy.

Despite the changes and uncertainties, adolescence quietly became the period in which I began building the muscles of resilience. Psychologists define resilience as the capacity to bounce back, adapt, recover, and regulate emotions in the face of adversity. My coping strategies – taking quiet responsibility, staying composed, and managing what I could – were early expressions of that. Even when I had no control over the larger world, I learned I could still manage parts of it.

Looking back, those early experiences became the foundation for everything that followed. They taught independence, yes – but also empathy, both for myself and for others. Like living without a diagnosis, resilience isn't defiant or dramatic; sometimes it's simply the act of enduring, the steady decision to keep moving forward one imperfect piece at a time. Every small act of coping, every moment of self-reliance, wove itself into the fabric of who I am today.

Self-crafted affirmations:

Drawn from my own experiences and growth — each one is a personal reminder, shaped by lessons learned, challenges faced, and moments of self-discovery.

- Every experience holds a lesson; wisdom is there if I choose to see it.

- Every day has a value and gives an opportunity to honour where you've come from.

- Life is a journey, not a destination. Embrace every step.

- Uncertainty is a teacher, not a threat.

- Challenges are opportunities for growth.

- I am enough, exactly as I am, in this moment.

- My strength is measured by persistence, not perfection.

SIX

KNOWLEDGE IS POWER

As I STEPPED INTO ADULTHOOD, the quiet lessons of resilience I had cultivated became my compass. Endurance, patience, and self-reliance – skills honed long before I fully understood their importance – were suddenly called upon in new ways. Life demanded more of me than I had faced before, but I carried the understanding that persistence didn't always look heroic; it often lived in small, repeated acts of commitment, in showing up when it would have been easier to retreat.

Education became a tangible arena in which to apply these lessons. I was the first in my family to attend university, stepping into a world that felt simultaneously exciting and overwhelming. On the surface, it might have appeared as ambition or intellectual curiosity – but in reality, it was survival. Every assignment, every exam, every late-night study session carried the weight of my upbringing. I had grown up witnessing the consequences of instability and financial stress, and I was determined to carve a life that offered independence, choice, and agency.

At school, I was an average student – I was never at the top of the class and rarely caused trouble. School was my refuge from my home life. Among friends, there were no questions about family struggles, no probing for explanations I couldn't give. We laughed, shared moments, and distracted ourselves together. Looking back, those hours of normalcy were formative – they were another way I learned to cope, to find pockets of stability and comfort amid the uncertainty of life.

Starting university after Year 12 felt impossible – financially, practically, and conceptually. My parents were unable to guide me; I would be the first in my family to navigate this journey. There was no roadmap. My only certainty was a desire to build a life on my own terms, to figure out how to navigate the world without a blueprint handed down from someone else. In fact, I wasn't even interested in university. All I wanted was to get a job, earn money, and gain my independence.

Opportunity came unexpectedly. Near the end of Year 12, I came down with tonsillitis – again – and needed surgery, causing me to miss a key job interview for a business administration traineeship at a national scientific organisation. I was disappointed – but fate offered a second chance. When the first round of interviews didn't yield a suitable candidate, applications reopened, and I attended an interview. I got the job.

That traineeship changed everything. I was immersed in a world of curiosity, knowledge, and mentorship. Surrounded by scientists and professionals who were passionate, generous, and endlessly encouraging, I began to see the transformative power of education. I learned that learning was not just about acquiring facts – it was about cultivating resilience, critical thinking, and self-confidence. I can trace the roots of my work ethic and self-belief directly to those early days, when I learned the value of showing up, asking questions, and trusting that I belonged even when I sometimes felt out of place.

During my traineeship, I took a second job at a hardware store to make ends meet, working nights on top of my full-time role. I was paying for car expenses, outings with friends, and board at home, so every dollar mattered. Some nights, I stood at the register in intense endometriosis pain, forcing a smile while serving customers, trying to focus through fatigue and the relentless ache. Each transaction, each polite interaction, felt like a small act of survival. And yet, those nights reinforced the quiet resilience I had been cultivating since childhood; the same skills of self-management, problem-solving, and pacing myself that had carried me through earlier challenges became the tools that allowed me to navigate the adult world, even when my body demanded I stop.

By the end of my traineeship, I had acquired 12 months of professional experience in administration and earned a Certificate III in Business Administration. I was offered a full-time position and chose to continue my business studies independently, completing a Certificate IV in Business Administration, followed by a Diploma in Business Administration. For over 10 years, I remained with the organisation, taking on multiple full-time roles and consistently challenging myself to grow, all while pursuing part-time study during evenings and weekends.

I achieved some significant milestones during that time, including buying my first house at age 21 – a moment I still look back on with pride. For someone who had grown up with financial limitations, it was more than just a property – it was independence, achievement, and proof that I could build a life on my own terms. I poured myself into making the space my own, and it was in shaping the garden that I discovered a new passion. The act of planning, planting, and nurturing brought me a sense of control, creativity, and calm that I hadn't experienced elsewhere. The garden became a canvas where I could experiment, solve problems, and watch the results of care and attention unfold over time.

This growing fascination naturally led me to formal studies in horticulture. I wanted to understand how design and structure could transform outdoor spaces. During my studies, I was selected to create a garden for the Avenue of Achievable Gardens Competition at the 2006 Melbourne International Flower and Garden Show – a showcase of affordable, water-efficient gardens designed and built by horticulture students.

My garden, Surrey Views, was inspired by the charm of a traditional English garden. Take-home brochures were developed for visitors, complete with a planting list, garden layout, and construction details so they could recreate it at home. Seeing my concept come to life at such a well-known event felt surreal – especially with a team helping me build it.

Of course, not everything went smoothly. Partway through construction, a nursery manager informed me that the correct materials for the stone wall cladding hadn't been delivered, and that it couldn't be installed. No alternatives were offered. I could've given up, but this display meant far too much to me. So, I found my own solution: I drove to the nearest store, asked for a cement-based adhesive, then returned – long after everyone else had gone home – and tiled the wall in fading daylight, having absolutely no idea whether what I was doing would work. But it did. The wall stood strong for the entire show.

The more I learned about landscape design, the more I wanted to apply it professionally. I started a small landscape design business on the side, helping clients create gardens that reflect beauty, balance, and sustainability. It was a way to merge creativity with knowledge, and to see tangible results from both my effort and learning.

It was towards the end of my Diploma in Horticulture, at age 26, that I bought my first horse – an experience that transformed my world in ways I hadn't anticipated. Circumstances soon led me to rescue another horse that was critically ill and in urgent need of surgery. She was surrendered to Mark and me in dire condition, with the hope that we could save her. Together, we transported her for life-saving surgery and watched the entire operation from an upstairs viewing room. She survived.

The months that followed were consumed by intensive rehabilitation – long days spent caring for her, monitoring her progress, learning how her body and mind responded, and adapting routines to support her recovery. Witnessing firsthand the knowledge, patience, and understanding required to nurture her back to health ignited a deeper curiosity in me. I became captivated by equine biology, behaviour, and welfare, eager to understand and support these remarkable animals on a profound level.

It was this experience – the prolonged, hands-on process of helping her recover – that inspired me to pursue a Bachelor of Equine Science, where I developed a thorough understanding of how to care for and support horses across all facets of the equine industry. I came to realise that much of the equine world was harsh, unnatural, and human-centred – managed in ways that disregarded their natural behaviours and welfare. I knew I wanted to do things differently.

During my degree, I began volunteering with an equine welfare organisation, investigating reports of neglect and providing short-term care that often grew into long-term rehabilitation. Many of the horses I encountered had been abused, neglected, and never taught basic handling skills such as being led, having their feet trimmed, or wearing a rug. Their defensive reactions, such as kicking during hoof care, were often misunderstood as "bad behaviour". In reality, these responses stemmed from fear and a lack of trust, not malice. They weren't stubborn or problem horses – they had simply never been shown patience, consistency, or gentle guidance. Each horse I rehabilitated still holds a special place in my heart; I remember them all vividly. Some with fractures, others battling severe laminitis – a painful, often fatal inflammation of the hooves – or the effects of long-term malnutrition, and I poured everything I had into helping them recover.

I eventually reached a point in my degree where I felt completely lost. For years, the course had been heavily science-based, and hadn't yet touched on the practical horse-focused subjects that had drawn me in from the start. Residential schools were in Wagga Wagga, New South Wales – five hours from home – and I recall sitting on the sandy riverbank on my own with a pen and paper writing pros and cons: continue or withdraw from my degree. Science was challenging at the best of times, and I wasn't sure if pushing through would be worth it. But quitting isn't in my nature. Seeing my thoughts laid out in front of me made the decision clear: I needed to finish what I'd started. I just needed a different way forward.

So I decided to take a 12-month break from my equine science degree and complete a Diploma of Equine Podiotherapy instead – motivated by a desire to help rescue horses in my care regain trust and allow their feet to be handled, so that I could restore proper hoof balance. Expecting a farrier to take on that kind of foundational training isn't realistic – they're paid to trim hooves, not to rebuild confidence in traumatised or unhandled horses.

The qualification required travelling to residential school in North-East Victoria – 100 km from home – along with extensive theory, hands-on training, and detailed case studies. I still had horses to care for each morning and night, so I made the daily return trip so I could continue fulfilling those responsibilities.

Throughout the course, I gained a far deeper understanding of equine anatomy and holistic hoof care, and an enormous respect for the skill and patience hoof trimmers and farriers bring to their work. But more than anything, it gave me practical tools to help rescue horses – especially those who had every reason to mistrust humans – to rebuild confidence, improve their soundness, and transform both physically and emotionally.

Once I learned to recognise when care was needed and respond accordingly, it became impossible to ignore elsewhere. While travelling through rural areas, I frequently encountered injured wildlife, particularly kangaroos struck by cars. More than once I found animals still alive that nobody had stopped for. I would spend hours waiting for wildlife volunteers to arrive and assess whether a humane end was the kindest option. I remember sitting beside a kangaroo with two broken legs as it tried, helplessly, to crawl back into the bush. That long, gruelling wait made me think: *I could do more.* So

I trained as a wildlife volunteer to ensure timely, compassionate care. The next training session happened to fall on my birthday – *Perfect*, I thought. It felt like a gift that would continue to give. Since then, I've cared for kangaroos, wombats, echidnas, birds, lizards, and turtles – animals in urgent need of help, whether that meant transport to a vet or, at times, the kinder act of euthanasia.

After returning to complete my equine science degree, I pushed through the final years of study with focus and determination. When I graduated, I felt the need to let my hair down and do something bold – something that would shake up the routine after years of study and hard work. Science had never come easily to me; I had to dive deep into extra reading and research just to grasp the concepts. I began searching for scientific volunteer opportunities – not just in Australia, but around the globe – eager to apply everything I had learned and put my hard-earned skills into practice.

A few options appeared, but none truly excited me – until I came across a two-week videography volunteer role at a scientific research station in the Amazon rainforest. The moment I saw it, something inside me ignited. I knew instantly this was it. I was beyond excited. I turned to Mark and said, "I'm going to the Amazon." He barely blinked; by then, he was used to my wild ideas. I completed my application and submitted it.

Weeks later, I received confirmation that I'd been accepted and was invited for a video call with the program director. Because of the station's remote location, I had questions about medical support and staying in contact with home. Access to medical care would be extremely limited, and there would be no way to communicate with family while I was there. I accepted the challenges and made a deal with

Mark: I would contact him when I arrived in Peru and again when I was departing. In between, I would be completely unreachable.

It took three days of travel to reach Puerto Maldonado, Peru, where I met the small group I'd be volunteering with. Our accommodation was a share house – with tarantulas crawling on the outside walls. I was equally nervous and exhilarated. I'd travelled before, but never alone, and never somewhere so remote. Thankfully, everyone spoke English and welcomed me straight away.

The next day, we set off for the research station – hours by car to reach the river, followed by a long boat ride deep into the heart of the jungle. I spent two weeks there, filming and assisting various research teams made up of volunteers from all around the world. I was the only Australian in the group. We embarked on night expeditions, the jungle alive with reflective eyes under torchlight, tracking animals and recording vital data: species, size, sex, and capturing small caimans (small-sized crocodiles) for study. Every effort was in service of protecting the rapidly vanishing Amazon rainforest that was threatened by rampant logging. Living there meant being immersed in it completely.

My bed rested on an open-air deck in the rainforest – no walls, just a mosquito net for protection. Each morning, I woke at first light to the calls of monkeys echoing through the canopy as they leapt effortlessly from branch to branch. Daily life involved constant vigilance: checking the bed for deadly spiders, inspecting shoes for tarantulas, and scanning my skin for ticks. I discovered two ticks nestled into my skin and crossed paths with a snake or two on my way to the outdoor bathroom. The whole experience was wild.

As part of my videography project, I learned that the nearby village of Lucerne was hosting a community event. I arranged a boat ride to capture it on film, but when I arrived, the village was eerily quiet – there was no sign of any gathering. With some broken English, a local explained it would start "soon". It never did. So I sat and watched village life unfold. Women cooking over fires, men hauling in enormous catfish from the river, and children playing. Two young girls were fascinated by me – the only Westerner in sight. They giggled, ran their fingers through my blonde hair, and examined my camera equipment with wide-eyed curiosity.

For hours I quietly observed, took photos, and soaked in the rhythm of life in a remote Amazonian village. I felt peaceful, grounded, and safe. It was one of those rare moments when time slows down and everything feels exactly as it should be. An unforgettable experience that still lives vividly in my memory.

When I returned home, I drew on what I had learned during my equine science degree to establish a small-scale agistment facility on the 20-acre property Mark and I had purchased – a place where horses could be cared for and grazed on quality pasture. The facility allowed me to focus on natural behaviours, welfare, and education, creating an environment where horses could thrive physically, mentally, and emotionally, free from unnecessary stress or exploitation.

This period of my life reinforced a lesson I had come to understand repeatedly: life doesn't follow a straight path. Rescuing a sick horse unexpectedly became the catalyst for an entire career and academic pursuit. The twists and turns – sometimes painful, sometimes inspiring – taught me that passion often emerges in response to circumstance, and that purpose can be discovered in the most unexpected ways.

In the early stages of my equine science degree, I worked full-time in higher education, specialising in marketing and student recruitment roles with multiple universities, requiring keen problem-solving, adaptability, and seamless collaboration in a fast-paced, high-pressure environment. Many positions also involved frequent interstate and international travel, adding further complexity and responsibility. Managing chronic illness on top of these responsibilities added a layer of complexity: navigating flights, long workdays, and deadlines while my body frequently had its own agenda. The experience was exhausting, yet it reinforced my determination to show up, adapt, and perform to the best of my abilities.

Over time, however, the cumulative demands of work, study, travel, and illness caught up with me, leading to burnout. I had stopped doing all the things I loved; life felt monotonous – like Groundhog Day. As a psychology student, the importance of self-care is constantly reinforced. Not just a professional requirement in a field known for emotional intensity, but a scientific necessity: research shows that consistent self-care practices regulate the nervous system, reduce cortisol levels, and protect against fatigue. Learning to prioritise wellbeing isn't indulgence – it's a form of prevention, both for ourselves and for those we aim to support.

Exhaustion and the feeling of being stretched too thin became constant companions. I struggled for a long time before realising that nothing would change unless I made a deliberate choice to change it. I reduced my level of commitment to my volunteer roles, quit my job and found a marketing consultant role close to home, which saved me hours of travel every day. It was during the COVID-19 pandemic, when I had acquired more personal time, that I discovered a new spark. Out of curiosity and a desire to reconnect with something meaningful, I began studying psychology. What started as personal interest quickly grew into passion. I thrived while studying a graduate diploma, uncovering how insights into human behaviour, resilience, and mental health could be directly applied to navigating real-life challenges.

Building on this academic success, I went on to complete my psychology honours degree. By that time, I had transitioned into a role with a not-for-profit organisation, where I gained insight into the resilience required by emergency service workers, such as police officers and paramedics – people so vital in our community. For my honours thesis, I explored resilience in depth, examining predictive factors such as personality, coping strategies, and social connection among State Emergency Service volunteers nationwide.

But when I initially embarked on my honours degree, I felt out of my depth. Statistics, in particular, felt like an entirely foreign language – numbers danced across the page, and I spent far too many late nights staring at datasets being unable to make any sense of them. My thesis topic excited me, but the process of turning ideas into coherent research, analysing data, and writing in the expected academic style was daunting. Consulting a tutor became my lifeline – he helped me navigate the murky waters of research design, data interpretation, and academic writing. With his guidance, I slowly gained confidence, learned to wrestle the numbers, and began to see my thesis not as a beast, but as a challenge I could rise to – with a little patience, humour, and external help.

Successfully completing my psychology honours degree opened the door to the next stage of my journey in becoming a qualified psychologist: earning a high enough grade to secure a place in a Master of Professional Psychology – a thrilling yet intimidating prospect. I knew the minimum pass mark for all assessments was 70%. Even though I had consistently scored above this throughout my psychology studies, I found myself worrying about juggling work, life, and study, and questioning whether I was truly capable of keeping up. Supportive friends reminded me that not trying would leave me wondering. I decided to step forward, self-doubt and all. By this point, I had learned that failure wasn't something to fear – it was something to learn from. I had also learned that my best effort was enough. I was going to commit fully, give it everything I had, and if that wasn't enough, I would be okay with it. As an adult, there's always so much to juggle, and it's tempting to take the easy option and not try. But that's not how growth happens. So, I accepted the offer, ready to give it my all.

When I started, I was quietly surprised to find that my professional and personal experiences had prepared me well. I could connect theory to practice in ways others couldn't – so much of what we were learning, I had lived, tested, and experienced firsthand. I knew what anxiety felt like. I understood hopelessness. I recognised the weight of so many difficult emotions because I had been there – and I had found ways to navigate through them, often relying on strategies I had discovered on my own.

Reflecting on my adult life, a clear pattern emerges: life rarely unfolds according to plan. Buying my first house sparked a passion for landscape design. An encounter with an unwell horse led me to pursue a degree, which in turn launched an equine business. Years of persistence in the workplace, alongside the struggles and triumphs of part-time study, ultimately guided me into psychology – a career I could never have imagined as a teenager. These twists and turns reinforced a lesson I had learned long ago: growth is rarely linear. The skills we develop, the knowledge we seek, and the resilience we cultivate often help us find purpose in ways we could never predict.

Every choice – intentional or unplanned – wove together the fabric of my adult life. From balancing work, study, travel, and chronic illness, to rescuing and caring for horses and wildlife, to navigating higher education careers, to pursuing psychology. Each experience reinforced the importance of perseverance, reflection, and adaptability. Life may take unexpected twists, but resilience, curiosity, and the pursuit of knowledge provide the tools to navigate them with purpose and integrity. These lessons naturally shaped the direction of my aspirations, guiding me toward a life focused not just on personal growth, but on lifting others along the way.

My goal in life is to continually better myself and to help others become the best versions of themselves, by offering support, encouragement, and guidance. Ultimately, I want to leave this world a better place than I found it – through small acts of kindness, meaningful connections, and contributing in ways that make a lasting, positive impact. Life, to me, is about learning, giving, and creating waves that extend far beyond my own immediate sphere.

Lessons learned:

- **Growth begins when comfort ends.** True growth often begins at the edges of discomfort – the moments that challenge our beliefs, stretch our limits, and push us into unfamiliar territory. It's uncomfortable, but it's also where resilience and self-awareness develop.

- **Passions and interests guide the way.** The things that spark my curiosity often lead me toward purpose. When I follow what excites me, even in small ways, I align with a sense of meaning that sustains me through challenges and uncertainty.

- **Financial support is important, especially while studying.** Security creates space for focus. Having financial stability by working full-time allowed me to study and grow without the constant stress of striving for survival overshadowing my progress.

- **Embrace and appreciate the people who invest in me.** Those who believed in me left a lasting impression, and by actively nurturing these bonds with gratitude and reciprocity, I helped them grow stronger.

- **It's okay to fail. It's how I grow.** Failure is not a reflection of my worth but a teacher in disguise. Every setback carries information – about my limits, my patterns, and my strength to try again. Every failure is an opportunity to learn.

- **Celebrating milestones builds confidence.** Acknowledging progress, no matter how small, reinforces my drive and reminds me how far I've come, even when the journey ahead still feels long.

- **Self-discipline is more important than motivation.** Motivation comes and goes, but self-discipline keeps me moving when enthusiasm fades. Small, consistent actions build habits, particularly important when life gets hard.

• **Never compromise my health for my job.** Work is only one part of a full life. No achievement is worth sacrificing my physical or mental wellbeing for. I protect my boundaries and prioritise recovery – my health is the foundation for everything else.

• **Work hard but with purpose.** Hard work has taught me that progress is earned, not given – and that's what makes it meaningful.

SEVEN

GRIEF

Life has a way of testing us in ways that feel almost unbearable. Some moments force us to confront the fragility of existence, to reckon with loss, and to discover the hidden depths of our own resilience. I have faced such moments – moments that reshaped not only the course of my life but also my understanding of love.

I was 26 when Dad passed away. The grief that followed settled quietly into the crevices of my life, shaping me in ways I could not yet articulate. I carried it in silence, a private weight I did not share. As with many hardships before it, I internalised the pain, telling myself – and those around me – that I was fine. I wasn't. I went about my days as if everything were normal, while inside I was struggling to cope.

It wasn't until more than a decade later, while I was studying psychology and completing an assignment on post-traumatic stress disorder (PTSD), that the pieces began to fall into place. I recognised that I had been living with PTSD symptoms for years – avoidance, hypervigilance, and feeling emotionally flat – symptoms that had quietly governed my life. The trauma of losing Dad had left a mark so deep, so overwhelming, that confronting it directly felt impossible. I tried to hold it all together without burdening anyone – just like I did when I was younger. But that quiet strength I prided myself on was really avoidance in disguise, a way of keeping the pain at arm's length.

The day he died is etched into my memory in painful detail. Arriving at his unit and calling an ambulance. The fear in his eyes as he was taken away. I watched him in distress in the emergency department, monitors beeping as his heart faltered. Then he went into cardiac arrest and doctors rushed in to resuscitate him. Deciding on the quality of his life was heart-wrenching – assessing whether his brain and body were capable of a meaningful future, and knowing this choice was the difference between life and death. Then came the hollow, incomprehensible moment when I was told he had passed, despite their best efforts to stabilise him. Sitting by his lifeless body afterward in disbelief, tearfully saying goodbye. And walking away for the final time, knowing I'll never see or talk to him again.

I was shattered – in shock, unable to grasp the chain of events that had unfolded so suddenly. I remember getting home late, exhausted, standing at the end of the bed as the reality was still taking hold. I wept uncontrollably in the dark while Mark held me. No words needed. Grief has a way of hollowing you out in those moments – the world narrows, sounds fade, and all that remains is the ache of what's been lost. It's as if time stops, and you're suspended between disbelief and unbearable truth.

The support that followed moved me almost as much as the loss itself. The genuine concern, the empathy, the home-cooked meals, the flowers, the cards, the hugs, and the phone calls – all gestures of care that touched me deeply. Even the awkwardness of people not knowing what to say, afraid of saying the wrong thing, came from a place of kindness. Nearly 20 years on, those memories still stir emotion as if they happened yesterday. Alana and I clung to each other throughout – supporting one another the best we could, both stumbling our way through grief.

Looking back, I wish someone had looked past my rehearsed "I'm okay". I wish someone had checked in months later, even years later. My grief had become a carefully constructed performance: a script I used to avoid opening that raw, aching wound. Occasionally I spoke of it briefly, but I never really let my guard down. I'm able to cope much better these days. I can speak about it openly, and if emotion rises, I know that's okay. I once read that grief is driven by love, and that idea has stayed with me. It reminds me that the person I'm grieving for held a deep place in my heart – one that will never fade.

I will always cherish the time I had with Dad. Many assume the hardest days are Father's Day or Christmas – and of course, I think of him then. But more often, his absence is felt on the days that matter most to me, the milestones that mark life's progress. Moments like graduations, starting a new job, buying a house – days to share, to celebrate, to talk about – are the ones when I notice Dad's absence the most.

Take my 30th birthday, for example – it carried a quiet, unshakable sadness. Or my graduation from my equine science degree. The ceremony was held at a racecourse in Sydney, and I flew Mum and Alana up so they could join Mark and me to share the moment. It was a milestone that meant a great deal to me. I was the first in my family to graduate from university, having devoted seven years to part-time study while managing a full-time job, pouring immense effort and dedication into achieving this milestone. After the ceremony, we celebrated and took photos. Of course, I couldn't resist the cliché moment of throwing my fancy graduation hat into the air. That was when I really noticed Dad's absence. I knew he would have hugged me tightly and told me how proud he was. I missed his affection. Mum's expressions of pride were always much more reserved. But that afternoon, standing outside in the racecourse gardens, I looked at her and noticed the tears in her eyes. She didn't have to say anything. In that moment, I knew she was proud – a feeling I hadn't often sensed from her. It reminded me how fleeting and precious these moments of connection are, and how quickly life can shift.

Two decades later, grief returned in a different form. Mum was diagnosed with Alzheimer's, a degenerative brain condition that slowly erodes memory, reasoning, and personality, making even simple daily activities increasingly difficult. Merciless in its progression, the disease stripped away her independence, leaving her reliant on constant care and support as it gradually reshaped her world. Caring for someone with Alzheimer's requires simultaneous mourning for who they once were, while preparing for the inevitable.

At first, she began neglecting bills, mixing up days and appointment times, and repeating herself in conversation. Even simple tasks, like making a shopping list, became a struggle. Alana, Mum's sister Leanne, and I stepped in to help, guiding her through daily tasks. Despite our best efforts, it became clear that she required more care than we could provide, so we began navigating the often-complex healthcare system to ensure she received the support she needed.

The gravity of the situation became unmistakably clear when, one day, she became confused with her medications and accidentally took an entire batch at once. I had previously tried various strategies to help her manage her pills – different blister packs, labelling systems – but nothing was foolproof. Thankfully, Leanne, who happened to be visiting that day, noticed immediately and took her to the hospital as a precaution. Physically, the overdose did not cause serious harm, but the doctors observed her declining cognition. Over the following days, they conducted a series of assessments, asking practical questions such as how she would respond in a fire, and had her complete everyday tasks like making a cup of coffee and using the microwave. She was unable to perform these tasks successfully.

A family meeting was called at the hospital, attended by a doctor, a social worker, Mum, Alana, myself, Mark, and Mum's partner at the time, Steven. We felt it was essential that Mum be included in the conversation. The discussion centred on aged care – the hospital could no longer safely allow her to return home alone, so we needed to find an immediate solution. Alana arranged appointments and visited facilities with Mum to find a suitable place. Navigating the system was challenging; availability is limited, and you can't simply choose a facility and just move in. Fortunately, the facility that both Alana and Mum liked had an opening, allowing her to move in directly and avoid transitional care, which can be particularly confusing for someone living with Alzheimer's.

Interestingly, Mum never asked about her home, her car, or her belongings – it was as if they had completely vanished from her memory. Alana and I were also both relieved that she didn't resist moving into aged care, as that would have added another layer of emotional complexity. We supported her transition from the hospital and helped her settle into the new facility, which seemed pleasant and offered daily activities recommended by doctors to help keep her mind engaged. I knew Mum, though: she was a social butterfly, but not one for playing bingo. Over the years, Alana and I continued to support her health and navigate the aged care system as her condition gradually declined.

Visiting her was bittersweet. She was mostly content, often chatting about staff members who were characters in her eyes. Conversations were repetitive and often didn't make sense; questions like "What did you have for lunch today?" or "Did you do any activities this week?" no longer made sense to ask, as she wouldn't recall. She did, however, remember her excursions, particularly the ones with water views of Western Port Bay or Port Phillip Bay. Although it could be difficult to piece together her stories, she clearly enjoyed the excursions. Alana would also take her on day trips, either to her house or to the beach, and those moments brought her joy.

Leaving the aged care facility after each visit was always hard. Watching someone – family or not – gradually become a shadow of themselves is heartbreaking. Mum retained some humour and always knew who Alana and I were, but sometimes she offered no greeting at all. She was unaware of the date or time, had no sense of the facility's daily activities, and required help with showering and dressing. She had even forgotten how to use her phone, despite us providing one with large, pre-programmed buttons featuring our photos. I reflected on why my sadness was so profound during this time, realising that she existed in her own world and seemed content. I was simply grieving for the person she once was. And I was grieving for her loss of independence.

Several years after her diagnosis, Mum suddenly became critically ill. She was rushed to the hospital, and after thorough evaluation, the doctors determined she had a golden staph infection that had advanced to sepsis.

In the first few days, Alana and I took turns visiting her, balancing our own jobs and, in my case, farm work and study as well. Mum knew where she was and that she was gravely ill, but she was also deeply confused. She would pull at her tubes and oxygen mask, unable to fully grasp what was happening, and would struggle to articulate her thoughts or how she was feeling, due to her Alzheimer's. Sitting beside her, watching her struggle, was utterly heart-wrenching – she was so weak. Within days, she was moved into ICU. I'll never forget sitting beside her in ICU, watching her in distress and repeatedly asking, "Can you help me?" By that time, the doctors had begun hinting at a very poor prognosis. For days, Alana and I watched her deteriorate, navigating conversations with an infection specialist, a geriatrician, doctors, and nurses. I was utterly exhausted. Just three weeks earlier, I had undergone reconstruction of both jaws – they were broken, repositioned and secured with titanium plates and 26 screws – a planned surgery to correct my bite and open my airway. The recovery had been hard: swelling, bruising, pain, and the need to sleep upright to reduce discomfort. I was still struggling to speak, my face being still slightly swollen, and I was limited to a liquid diet. Hospital food wasn't an option, so I asked Mark to bring in protein shakes so I could get some nutrition. At that point, Alana and I were staying with Mum around the clock, and I was fully aware that my own body was still in the early stages of healing.

When Mark arrived, I met him in the hospital foyer. I collected my items and let him decide for himself whether he wanted to see Mum, gently warning him that it would likely be upsetting. After some consideration, he chose to come upstairs with me. Mark and I had been together for 25 years, and I could feel, without a word, the emotions stirring in him: a mix of empathy, uncertainty, and helplessness. He was already carrying the weight of his own dad's health struggles, and seeing Mum so vulnerable only added to that burden. When Mark and I walked into her room together, the reality of her fragility was undeniable, and the quiet tension between us spoke volumes.

Her fragility was impossible to ignore, and I found myself silently preparing for the hard conversations ahead. The geriatrician, who visited daily, was honest about the next steps, recommending palliative care. I agreed; seeing Mum suffer, knowing the seriousness of her infection, which had now also progressed to pneumonia, her chronic kidney disease, and the moderate-to-advanced Alzheimer's she was living with, I couldn't bear for her to endure any more distress. Alana took a little longer to come to terms with it. Mum was sometimes able to eat or drink, and Alana hoped these small signs might indicate improvement. But the doctors were clear: the infection was highly likely to overwhelm her body, and continued antibiotics would only prolong the inevitable. I completely understood where Alana was coming from – she loved Mum deeply and didn't want to let her go.

After many discussions with medical staff, we made the heart-wrenching decision to transition Mum into palliative care. Antibiotics were stopped, and palliative medications were started. From that moment, the process was harrowing. We stayed by her side constantly, unsure how long it would take for her organs to fail and for her to take her last breath. Leanne was there too. Sleep was scarce; we barely left the room.

At first, Mum would wake and become distressed. Over time, the nurses adjusted her medications to keep her calm and comfortable. Still, it didn't feel entirely peaceful – I couldn't know what she was experiencing. We listened to her laboured, gurgling breaths for hours. To us, her efforts looked like struggle, and it was profoundly upsetting to watch.

One night nurse stood out. She cared for Mum with such quiet dignity that we wanted to lock her in the room and never let her go. She fluffed pillows, straightened Mum's posture, smoothed her hair, added blankets – all with gentle, deliberate movements and genuine compassion. Moments like that matter most, when someone is nearing the end of life and entirely dependent on the care and presence of others. A head nurse also came by to explain what was happening, helping us understand the palliative process and make sense of the overwhelming grief of the preceding days. There were several moments when we thought Mum would pass. We cried, held her frail hands, said our goodbyes – only to laugh softly when she clung to life, and we whispered, "Mum, you're still here!"

To lighten the mood, Alana, Leanne, and I shared memories of old times – funny moments, the ones that make you laugh and smile. Alana and I joked as much as we could, a small shield against the intensity of what was unfolding. We played her favourite songs and artists – Jimmy Barnes, Aussie rock, old-school classics – anything to bring comfort, both to Mum and ourselves. Those small gestures – the music, the quiet attentiveness, the periodic laughter – became our way of honouring her and navigating the grief, fear, and helplessness that filled those final days.

Watching her decline forced me to reflect on what truly matters. Work and study are temporary, but who we are, how we love, and how we treat others endure. I asked myself, if I were in her position, who would be here? Who would witness my life and how I faced its end? I'll never know, but it clarified the values I strive to live by: kindness, integrity, genuineness, and love.

On the second day after discontinuing the antibiotics, in the early hours of the morning, Mum's breathing began to slow. It was the sign we'd been told to look out for – that the end was near. Alana and I were trying to get some rest in her room; we were both completely exhausted. I was awake, on "shift", while Alana had only just laid down. When I noticed Mum's breathing change, I called out to Alana. I wasn't sure if this was it, but I didn't want to risk her missing the moment. She was already asleep, so I gently nudged her awake.

We both sat up in the softly lit room, one on each side of Mum's bed. Her eyes were closed, her head tilted to one side. The pauses between each breath grew longer, each gasp followed by a normal breath before the next long silence. I knew, then, that this was it. We sat there, holding her hands, quietly present as an Aussie rock playlist played softly in the background.

When Mum took her final breath, the relief I felt was immense – no more suffering, no more distress or confusion, no more pain. She was free. But even with the knowledge that this day was inevitable, the ache mirrored exactly what I felt when Dad died. The world narrowed, sounds faded, and all that remained was the weight of loss. Time seemed to stop, leaving me suspended between disbelief and unbearable truth. Immediately after her passing, "Working Class Man" by Jimmy Barnes, one of her favourite artists, played. Coincidence, maybe, but to us it felt like her final farewell – a cheeky, heartfelt "thank you" and goodbye.

I texted close family and friends of her passing; I'd been keeping them updated throughout the week making phone calls only when I felt strong enough – though I know my friends wouldn't mind silence on the line. I called Mark and told him Mum had passed, then rang Leanne, who wanted to come and sit with her one last time.

Alana and I stayed with Mum for a little while longer. We'd said our goodbyes and were grateful to have been there for her final moments, so we felt at peace leaving when we did. When it was time to leave, we packed up our things. I was the last to step out of the room, pausing at the doorway to look back one last time. After the chaos and distress of the past few days, I didn't want those to be my final memories of her. I wanted to remember her as she was after she passed – peaceful, still, free of pain. I took in the image carefully, fixing it in my mind.

It was around 3 am when Alana and I left the hospital, got in our cars and drove home. The streets were quiet and empty. I felt hollow – waves of grief crashing, then fading into numbness. When I got home, I crawled into bed, turned away from Mark, and completely let go. All the exhaustion, trauma, and grief came pouring out – the anguish of watching Mum suffer, the weight of making impossible decisions, and the lingering pain from my own surgery. Mark held me without saying a word. None were needed.

In the days that followed, a familiar rhythm set in – much like after Dad's death. There was an outpouring of kindness and genuine care from family, friends and colleagues. Some people didn't mention Mum's passing unless I brought it up first – not out of avoidance, but compassion. They didn't want to say the wrong thing or cause more pain. Many instead asked about my surgery recovery, using it as a gentler way to check in. I understood; sometimes people just don't know what to say.

I was okay talking about Mum. If losing Dad taught me anything, it was the importance of speaking about grief rather than burying it. I didn't share for sympathy – I did it to release what sat heavy inside me instead of carrying it alone, like I used to. Still, the combination of grief, trauma, and physical recovery left me completely depleted. In the weeks that followed, my nervous system stayed on high alert – hypervigilant, emotional, and unable to rest. Remembering how poorly I'd coped after Dad died, I knew I had to take responsibility for myself this time – to use what I'd learned and actively tend to my own healing.

The sleep deprivation was relentless. I was wired and exhausted at the same time – too tired to function, yet unable to switch off. It felt as if my body was bracing for the next blow, the next trauma. I couldn't continue like that, so my GP prescribed sleeping tablets to help me finally get some rest. They provided a temporary reprieve, but I knew that pills alone couldn't reset a nervous system thrown into chaos. While they can induce sleep, sleeping tablets don't replicate the natural architecture or restorative processes of true sleep. Unlike natural sleep, which cycles through stages essential for nervous system regulation, memory consolidation, and hormonal balance, pharmacologically induced sleep can suppress deep slow-wave and REM stages, limiting its ability to restore the body and mind. The tablets offered immediate relief, but I understood they were only a short-term solution.

Through studying psychology, I had learned how profoundly trauma affects the body: the sympathetic nervous system

– the fight-or-flight response – can remain overactive long after the triggering event. My hyperalertness, fragmented sleep, jumpiness, low tolerance and emotional volatility were all signs of this. Recovery required intentional, sustained strategies: pacing myself, acknowledging limits, reintroducing structure, and practising self-compassion. It was painstaking work, rebuilt moment by moment.

Recovery didn't happen in isolation. I balanced work, study, and daily responsibilities while giving myself space to grieve. Small, deliberate actions became milestones: honouring fatigue, reintroducing gentle structure, paying mindful attention to my nervous system, and embracing quiet, restorative rhythms of daily life. There was no roadmap, no instruction manual. I had to experiment, try, and adjust. I focused on purposeful breathing multiple times a day, used calming sleep playlists, and sought quiet spaces away from noise, people, and movement. Slowly, over time, my system began to recalibrate, and I felt glimpses of myself returning.

Through these experiences, I learned that grief is not linear. It is unpredictable, consuming, and deeply intimate. Continuing to show up – at work, in study, in life – amid emotional and physical depletion is itself an act of courage. Recognising how trauma can dysregulate the nervous system helped me see that recovery and resilience are cultivated, not instantaneous – they demand patience, support, and conscious effort.

Reflecting on the deaths of my parents – so different in their timing, circumstances, and impact – reshaped me, reinforcing that resilience is not about avoiding pain, but about learning to live with it, integrate it, and to continue moving forward with intention, care, and love.

Reflections:

- Extreme life events can profoundly dysregulate the nervous system; grief, trauma, and physical stress combined intensify each other. Recovery takes time and intentional effort.

- Recovery requires patience, strategies, and sustained effort. Healing is rarely linear, and small steps matter.

- Grief comes from love. It is a testament to the significance of the person in my life.

Practical takeaways:

- **Honour my limits.** Recognise when my mind and body need rest. Extreme stress, trauma, or grief are likely to exceed my natural capacity, and ignoring these signals can lead to burnout. Pacing myself is not failure; it's a conscious act of self-preservation. Listening to my body's cues, taking breaks, and giving myself permission to step back when needed is essential. Small, consistent steps toward recovery are far more sustainable than forcing myself to keep going when I am at my limit.

- **Reconnect with my body.** Self-awareness is one of the most useful skills I've developed. I've come to understand through experience that trauma and grief can make me feel disconnected from my own body. Gentle movement like walking, stretching, or yoga, combined with mindful breathing and sensory grounding, helps regulate my nervous system and restore a sense of presence.

- **Prioritise sleep.** Sleep is foundational for both physical and emotional recovery. Even short naps, consistent bedtimes, or basic sleep hygiene practices – such as winding down before bedtime – support my nervous system regulation. Rest is not indulgent; it's essential for resilience, processing emotions, and maintaining cognitive clarity during difficult times.

- **Seek support.** Asking for help is not a weakness; it is a courageous and necessary act. Friends, family, or professionals can provide emotional buffering during intense grief or stress. Accepting support doesn't mean I am incapable – it means I am human. I'm learning to lean on others for practical help, emotional validation, or just simply ask them to be present in moments of struggle.

- **Respect grief.** Grief is deeply personal and unique. Comparing my experiences to others' or trying to adhere to societal expectations of "how to grieve" can be harmful. I honour my own process. By allowing myself to feel – whether it's sadness, anger, relief, or moments of joy, I do so with no judgement. My grief is my pathway, and it doesn't need to follow a timeline or pattern.

- **Embrace bravery.** Courage isn't about feeling no fear; it's about facing uncertainty and making difficult choices anyway. Facing the reality of Mum's illness, choosing palliative care, and navigating the emotional and practical complexities required bravery I didn't always feel. Courage showed up in making choices for her wellbeing, advocating on her behalf, and holding space for her, Alana, and myself through moments of fear, grief, and helplessness.

PART FOUR

ENDURANCE IN MOTION

EIGHT

HONOURING THE GOOD DAYS

How DID I GO FROM hating sport in high school to running ultra-trail marathons three decades later? Somewhere along the way, running became more than a physical pursuit – it became a reflection of the lessons life had already been teaching me. Each kilometre mirrored the resilience I'd built through experience of living with chronic illness, balancing work and study, and enduring personal loss. The qualities life demanded of me – patience, preparation, tolerance for discomfort, and reflection – proved just as essential on the trail as they were off it, turning every run into both a challenge and a lesson.

It was endometriosis that first sparked my passion for endurance running, transforming pain into purpose. On bad days, the pain was unbearable – hours curled up in bed, body clenched, mind consumed by waves of agony. I felt trapped, as though my life had been hijacked by a body I couldn't control. So on the good days, I moved. I ran. Each step felt like reclaiming lost ground. I was deeply grateful for the simple ability to move freely – to breathe without pain, to feel strength where weakness had lived. Running became an act of rebellion and renewal, a way to reclaim my body one stride at a time.

And with each progressively longer race, I learned that the only limits I truly had were the ones I allowed myself to believe.

Each race presented a new test, stretching me a little further, a little longer. The first few marathons taught me how to pace myself, how to endure, and how to summon strength when every part of me wanted to stop. With every subsequent race, the distance grew, the terrain became more unforgiving, and the stakes felt higher – not just physically, but mentally and emotionally. Just as life rarely gives you the same challenge twice, each run was different, forcing me to adapt, learn, and discover reserves I didn't know I had, teaching me that growth often comes from facing the unknown. My journey didn't start with ultramarathons or 100 km trail races – it began small, with manageable steps that slowly built confidence and curiosity.

In 2018, at the age of 37 – 10 months before my endometriosis diagnosis – I stepped out of a café in the Victorian seaside town of San Remo and noticed a flyer pinned to the window: an 8 km coastal run. Something about it drew me in. I wasn't a serious runner – just a few kilometres here and there – but the thought of pushing myself further sparked something. Eight kilometres was beyond my usual distance, yet it felt like the right kind of challenge. When I got home, I looked up the details, signed up, and felt an instant surge of excitement. I've always loved the ocean, and the idea of running along the coast in summer – my favourite season – felt like the perfect blend of freedom and fulfilment.

The event was everything I hoped it would be. The trail hugged the wild coastline, offering sweeping ocean views and sunlit cliffs. It wasn't easy – the heat was intense and the hills demanding – but the scenery made every step worth it. I had no structured training plan:

no cardio schedule, no strength work, no nutrition strategy. My plan was simple – just run. I finished in the front half of the field and felt an overwhelming rush of pride.

A few months later, I signed up for a half marathon (21 km) at Wilsons Promontory National Park – affectionately known as The Prom – the southernmost tip of mainland Australia, famed for its granite peaks, wild beaches, and untamed wilderness. I've always loved the outdoors; nature has a way of grounding me unlike anything else. I hadn't been to The Prom in years, but I still remembered its raw, rugged beauty. The idea of running through that landscape felt electrifying.

To prepare, I pieced together a basic training plan that I could adapt around work and study. I researched free templates online, read articles and advice from running websites, and scheduled sessions based on what felt sustainable. It felt good to have a daily fitness goal, something concrete to work toward. I even made a ritual of crossing off each session after completion, a small act that brought satisfaction. The truth, though, was that I had no idea what I was doing. I'd never set foot in a gym, had no formal fitness education, and didn't know a single runner – certainly not a trail runner. Trail elevation, VO_2 max, strength conditioning, cross training, hill repeats: none of it meant anything to me yet. I taught myself along the way, guided by curiosity, trial and error, and a stubborn determination to see what I was capable of.

The day before the race, Mark and I explored The Prom as the 100 km runners – mostly men who had set off the day before – came striding past. I watched them in awe. Running 100 km through that terrain seemed unimaginable; even driving that distance feels far.

Completing half a marathon felt challenging enough – a narrow single trail winding through rugged, uneven terrain – but I loved every minute of it. With only 40 runners, the crowd thinned quickly, leaving just me and nature. The course was demanding – steady climbs, roots and rocks waiting to trip me up, and the ever-present risk of not finishing. I'd had bad knees since my twenties, the crunch of worn cartilage a constant reminder of fragility, yet the trail made me feel strong and alive. Navigation became part of the test too: scanning for small flags to stay on course, all while carrying mandatory gear – a phone, water, a first aid kit with a snake-bite bandage, a waterproof jacket, gloves, a beanie, and sun protection. Even for a shorter race, the added weight made the challenge feel real.

For all the physical pain, it was worth it – the rawness, the solitude, the rhythm of breath. Every so often I stopped to take photos or simply stand still and take it all in: the vastness, the peace, the reminder that I was still here, still capable. Dad had been gone a few years by then, and as I crossed the finish line, I thought about how proud he'd be. Almost immediately, though, my body began to seize – muscles stiffening with each step. I remember pacing the car park, laughing through the pain, telling Mark, "I can't stop moving or my legs and glutes will seize up!"

Six months later, my endometrioma ruptured, leading to the mistaken appendicitis diagnosis and removal of my appendix, and soon after, my first laparoscopy. Looking back, it's astonishing to realise what my body had been enduring all that time – organs fused together by endometrial tissue – yet somehow it still carried me through two running events. Recovery from my surgeries was tough, but those memories became my anchor. If I could complete a half marathon on rugged terrain when my body was struggling, what might I be capable of now, given a fresh start?

One year later, fully recovered from surgery, I was ready for a new challenge. I signed up for a marathon on Mt Baw Baw – 44 km with more than 4,000 metres of climbing and descent. This time, it wasn't just about running – it was about proving to myself that I could rebuild, that I could trust my body again.

Without a coach or running community, I became my own guide, crafting a training plan through research, trial and error, and intuition. Years of study and professional experience had honed my discipline, persistence, and capacity to learn – all of which I poured into my preparation. Each completed session brought structure and purpose, strengthening my body and steadying my mind.

The day before the event, Mark and I set up camp an hour from Mt Baw Baw with our rescue dogs, Jet and Roxy. Race-day preparation was anything but glamorous – no creature comforts, no warm room to retreat to, and an outdoor bathroom. I woke before dawn, ate a simple breakfast, grabbed my running pack with my mandatory gear, drove up the mountain in the dark, and stretched in the car park at first light. Around me, the other runners – mostly men, fit and seasoned – moved with effortless confidence, and I felt a flicker of doubt. I didn't feel like I belonged. But I reminded myself: *I've earned my place.*

The course was brutal – rocky escarpments, endless climbs, and narrow, twisting trails. To cope, I broke the distance into segments: 10 km at a time, five if I had to. When even that felt like too much, I went smaller still – step by step, breath by breath. *Just keep moving forward*, I'd tell myself. Sometimes I picked visual markers too: *Just get to that tree* or *Just make it to that ridgeline.* Fuelling was another challenge. I'd packed muesli bars and lollies, not yet realising how crucial proper nutrition was for endurance. By the 30 km mark, everything hurt – toes, hips, knees – but I used the memory of endometriosis as my power. I'd ask myself, *Is this pain worse than endometriosis?* The answer was always no.

I finished second female. There was no crowd and no fanfare – just a few volunteers clapping as I crossed the line. And somehow, that felt perfect. Growing up, I learned to be my own biggest supporter: to celebrate quietly, wholeheartedly, from within. Recognising and honouring my own wins – even when no one else is watching – is what I believe to be one of the foundations of inner strength.

Mt Baw Baw cemented my love for trail running – the connection with nature, the solitude, the grit required to keep going when everything in me wanted to stop, and the sheer rawness of it all. Out there in the mountains, often alone for hours with no one in sight, I felt profoundly grateful. After everything – illness, surgery, setbacks – I could move, breathe, and run. That, in itself, felt like the greatest victory of all.

What I felt intuitively on those trails, researchers are now articulating more clearly. Emerging research has highlighted the psychological benefits of ultra-trail and endurance running, particularly in trauma recovery. Studies suggest that the physical intensity and prolonged duration of these events can activate adaptive stress-response mechanisms, promoting emotional regulation, resilience, and post-traumatic growth. The repetitive, rhythmic nature of running can induce a meditative state that supports emotional processing, while the natural environments typical of trail running enhance grounding and reduce stress. Ultra-endurance athletes often show higher pain tolerance, mental toughness, and heightened self-awareness – traits that overlap with adaptive coping strategies seen in trauma recovery. For many, long-distance running offers both a physical outlet and a framework for rebuilding trust in the body after trauma – restoring a sense of agency and inner stability. When I first came across this research, it resonated deeply. It may not hold true for every ultra-runner, but it certainly did for me.

My next challenge came a year later in 2021, in the Victorian high country: a marathon that included Mt Feathertop – Victoria's second-highest peak – promising both breathtaking views and punishing climbs. Mark and I turned it into another weekend adventure, camping at the local caravan park in Harrietville, the town where the race would start. Nestled quietly in the valley, framed by towering mountains, and shaped by a river winding through the park, the town was nothing short of beautiful.

On race morning, I woke around 5 am, the stiffness in my body a reminder of the lack of glamour in pre-race camping. I ate breakfast, stretched, and walked to the start line where about 40 runners were gathering. Among them, I felt small – a little out of place and undeniably nervous. I've come to see nerves as a signal, not a flaw: my body's way of telling me that something truly matters. When we care deeply about what lies ahead, the sympathetic nervous system kicks in, sharpening focus, heightening alertness, and priming us to perform. Nervousness wasn't a weakness; it was readiness in disguise.

At 6 am, we set off into the darkness, head torches glowing. The morning was perfectly still. There were no cheering crowds, no traffic, no conversations, just the soft, synchronised sound of feet striking bitumen. The rhythm was profound enough to give me goosebumps

– strangely soothing in its simplicity. Soon after, we turned onto a dirt road and began the first gruelling climb.

As the sun rose, snippets of conversation floated between runners – words of encouragement, quick check-ins, those small gestures of shared humanity I've come to cherish in endurance running. The ascent to Mt Feathertop was punishing; my quads burned, my lungs protested, but eventually I reached the summit. The wind howled, fog pressed in close, and I could barely see a few metres ahead. Not the view I'd hoped for, but I'd made it. I paused to absorb the moment before continuing across the mountain ranges to Razorback Ridge, a narrow alpine trail linking Mt Feathertop to Mt Hotham – one of the most iconic and dramatic ridges in Victoria, exposed and panoramic, demanding attention at every step.

On my way down Mt Feathertop, the fog and bad weather lifted, and by the time I reached the ridge, the world unfolded before me: endless ridgelines, sun-drenched peaks, deep valleys stretching into the distance. It was breathtaking – the kind of beauty that humbles you, reminding you of both your smallness and your place in something vast. Yet the same trail that inspired awe demanded absolute vigilance. One misstep could have serious consequences, and help would be hours away – if you were even in a state to receive it. That danger sharpened every moment, making each footfall an act of full presence. Trail running, I realised, is as much about awareness and respect for nature as it is about endurance.

That constant need for focus and presence still left room for reflection. Sometimes I thought deeply about things, finding that reflection helped me process emotions and gain clarity. Other times, I thought of nothing at all. Often, I simply listened – to nature, the rhythm of my feet, my breath, or music. I experimented with all kinds of genres: slower, yoga-like tracks that calmed and centred me; grunge or rock that fuelled grit; electronic and dance tunes that propelled me forward. Just as in everyday life, music had a profound effect on my mood on the trail, boosting motivation and reducing perceived effort. Upbeat, rhythmic tracks energised my body, sharpened focus, and created a sense of flow, making even the toughest runs feel exhilarating, while slower, meditative music helped me tune into my breath and movement with calm awareness. Music became my companion, shaping the emotional landscape of each kilometre and grounding me through the intensity of the terrain.

A few kilometres from the finish, despite the focus and rhythm I'd found in the music, I slipped and hit the ground. I got up, checked myself over – nothing broken, nothing sprained – and kept moving. I couldn't help but laugh. *Welcome to trail running*, I thought. Falls are part of the deal; I'd gone down plenty of times before, tripping over roots, rocks, and perfectly camouflaged sticks. Constantly scanning for hazards is exhausting, and it only takes a split second of inattention for things to go wrong – especially as fatigue sets in. Yet when I finally crossed the finish line, eighth female overall, the sense of accomplishment was overwhelming. Every cut, bruise, stumble, and moment of focus had led to that one unforgettable triumph.

But as proud as I was, I had no idea what the mountains still had in store for me. A year later, the Mt Buller marathon would test me to my core. By the 30 km mark, during the long climb up Mt Buller from the valley floor, the weather shifted. Fog rolled in – thick and damp – clinging to my clothes and chilling me despite the heat of the climb. I was stuck in a maddening cycle: the uphill effort made me sweat, but any pause brought an instant, biting cold. My waterproof jacket did little; my thermal layers were already damp. Getting my clothes wet in the first place was a huge mistake, and at the time, I had no idea how serious that could become.

As I climbed higher, lightheadedness crept in. Something felt wrong. When I glanced at my watch, I realised I was unlikely to make the cut-off. Unhelpful thoughts settled over me like a weight: *I don't want to do this anymore. I want to give up. I'm too tired.* My body felt as though it was struggling, even beginning to shut down.

Eventually, I reached a clearing with ski lifts – and there, the course flags shot sharply upward, marking a near-vertical line up a brutal ski run. I froze. I felt completely defeated – body and spirit. Staring up at that climb, all I wanted was to quit. But there was no one around. No way back. No help. Only forward and straight up.

Step by agonising step, slower than a sloth on a lazy Sunday, I inched upward, and grappled with the idea that I was unlikely to finish. My time was long gone; I was sure I was out of the race. Every footfall became an act of stubbornness, every breath a negotiation with my mind. Eventually, I reached the top and saw the next check-in station. Head down, pace crawling, I braced myself for the volunteer to tell me I was done. But she clapped and said, "Keep going, love!" Shocked, I asked, "I'm not out?" She smiled. "No! Keep going!" And just like that – the overwhelming desire to quit, so strong only minutes before, lifted. I kept going, one foot in front of the other.

As I descended toward Mt Buller village, the fog thickened again, dampness soaking through my clothes and chilling me to the bone. Shivering, I grew increasingly desperate. I knew my body was struggling, and I needed to reach some form of civilisation – fast.

When I finally crossed the finish line – fourth female, last in a group of 25, three of whom hadn't finished – I felt satisfied, but I could sense how slow and depleted my body was from the cold. Fifteen minutes later, as we drove down the mountain, my breathing changed rapidly. I began to hyperventilate.

Mark turned the car around and drove me back to Mt Buller village for medical treatment. I was experiencing mild hypothermia and was instructed to strip off my wet clothes, wrap myself in a space blanket – a thin, reflective sheet designed to retain body heat – and eat something. Within minutes, I began to recover. It was a visceral reminder that no finish line, no summit, no personal triumph matters if I don't put my body first. Endurance isn't just about strength or grit – it's about respecting limits, educating myself, listening to the signs, and honouring myself enough to survive to run another day. I was fortunate to escape unscathed, but the lesson stayed with me. Once wet and chilled, the body's core temperature can drop rapidly, and without immediate action, hypothermia can become a serious, even life-threatening risk – a reality to respect in mountainous terrain where the weather can change in an instant. That's why competitors carry mandatory gear, to withstand all conditions and situations, but it's equally vital to know how and when to use it.

After several trail marathons, curiosity pushed me to test myself on the road – the Noosa Marathon in Queensland. Training felt different this time: fewer hills, more focus on pace and distance. I'd learned much more about nutrition, hydration, and recovery – though I made one major training mistake by pushing through hip pain during a 25 km training run on concrete. The pain lingered for months, and I promised myself never to train long distances on concrete again.

The weekend in Noosa was calm and peaceful – sunshine, ocean swims, long coastal walks. Race day was the opposite: electric and full of energy. The streets buzzed with runners and twice as many supporters, a completely different atmosphere from the quiet solitude I was used to on the trails. The route wound around Noosa on bitumen, in a multi-lap format. I held my pace, but near 30 km, lactic acid settled in and I slowed. On the final lap, my watch told me I wouldn't break four hours – but the finish line arrived sooner than expected. The final stretch was lined with cheering spectators, their voices lifting exhausted runners toward the end. My legs felt like lead, yet when I heard strangers calling my name – "Come on, Bec, you've got this!" – the pain dissolved. I crossed the finish line in just under four hours – proud, sore, and smiling. It was a strong run and a great experience, but it didn't give me the same satisfaction as the trails. I already knew the truth. Road running wasn't my thing: it was the trails I loved.

From there, my distances grew steadily: first 50 km along Victoria's rugged Surf Coast, then an 80 km event through the bush and sands of Margaret River in Western Australia. With each finish line, my confidence grew, as did my understanding of what my body and mind were capable of. It wasn't just about accumulating kilometres – it was about building resilience, deepening my knowledge of training and recovery, and honing the self-discipline that had carried me through years of challenges. Every race became a reminder of how far I had come, both physically and personally, and of the quiet strength I could summon when I committed fully to a goal.

Those long, solitary hours on the trails became my meditation. I fell, stumbled, pushed through exhaustion, and kept going. I learned the hard way that sand running is brutal, yet I found peace in the wilderness – the valleys, ridgelines, forests, and oceans that surrounded me. Every race became both an adventure and a form of healing, proof that endurance and beauty can coexist. My training evolved too. I learned from mistakes, gradually building my understanding of fitness and what it takes to prepare for challenging terrain. I studied trail courses, considered elevation and environmental conditions, and trained accordingly.

One thing I knew for certain: podiums were never my goal. Even when I finished in a respectable position, my victories were quieter and more personal – finishing strong, making the cut-off, simply crossing the line at all. But with each event, something was shifting. I thought back to Wilsons Prom, to the day I watched those men tackle the 100 km course and marvelled at what the human body could endure. Back then, it had seemed unimaginable – almost impossible. Yet a spark had been lit: *Maybe that could be me.* Could I push myself that far? One hundred kilometres – just 20 more than my last race.

I began searching for 100 km events that would fit around work, study, farm life, and my preference to avoid training through cold, wet winters. Months later, I found it: a 100 km, two-day trail run in Victoria's high country, advertised as Australia's toughest trail run. Even better, the entry fees supported children with autism. *This is it,* I thought. Without a moment's hesitation, I signed up.

NINE

TRAINING GROUND

Peak performance doesn't come from sheer willpower alone; it's built gradually – step by step, kilometre by kilometre – through months of structured training, intentional recovery, and attention to both nutrition and mindset. Every long run, every hill repeat, every gym session teaches the body to adapt, to sit with discomfort, and to function under stress. There's a saying ultramarathon runner and motivational speaker, Nedd Brockmann, shares often: "Get comfortable being uncomfortable." I repeated it constantly – during the final few reps at the gym when fatigue set in, on the spin bike when my quads burned, or grinding up a hill when my lungs were on fire. It's hard. It never becomes easy. But learning to lean into that discomfort, rather than resist it, is what transforms both body and mind. With that foundation, the mountains and long, unforgiving distances ahead stop feeling like threats and start becoming challenges you're equipped to meet.

I developed a four-month training program combining all aspects – strength, endurance, nutrition, and mindset. These layers didn't just prepare me for the 100 km event; they formed a base that allowed me to enjoy the process too. Several times a week, I hit the gym to build overall strength, with a focus on the stabilising muscles that keep me balanced on uneven terrain and shield me from injury. Slow-twitch muscle fibres – those responsible for endurance – were a major focus, helping improve fatigue resistance and efficiency over long distances. Every six to eight weeks, my personal trainer, Mel, would reset my program to keep the load progressive and my body adapting.

My schedule was intense. I kept everything in a colour-coded spreadsheet – precise, detailed, mapped out from morning to night. Key sessions in the morning, key sessions in the afternoon, seven days a week. Even rest days weren't truly rest: yoga, long walks, or water sports kept me moving without overloading my body. By the end of the training block, I had accumulated more than 600 km across long runs, easy runs, hill repeats, and speed sessions. The increase in volume was slow and deliberate. I wasn't willing to risk injury, and a sports physio once taught me a formula that stuck: if your acute workload – the sudden jump in training – increases beyond 1.75 times a week, your injury risk roughly doubles. In other words: push too fast, too soon, and your body pays for it. So I built everything methodically. No shortcuts. In week one, I ran 11 km total. By week 14, I was running 130 km, split across two back-to-back long sessions. And in the final two weeks, I tapered – easing the load so my body could repair, restore, and arrive at the start line ready.

Nutrition was equally essential. It's what kept my body capable of enduring such extreme distances. Carefully timed carbohydrates, proteins, and electrolytes helped maintain blood glucose levels, supported muscle repair, and prevented excessive fatigue. With the right fuel delivered at the right moments, the body becomes astonishingly capable.

The whole process taught me something fundamental: nothing worthwhile comes easily. Fitness is earned. People often see the finish line, but the real story lies in the quiet, repetitive, disciplined steps long before you ever get there.

While physical preparation can take you far, it's mental grit that carries you through the toughest moments. Running 100 km is as much a psychological battle as a physical one. Doubt, fatigue, discomfort – they're constant companions. Techniques like visualisation, positive self-talk, and breaking long runs into small, manageable fragments help me stay present. Leaning into the discomfort instead of fearing it turns each challenge into a marker of progress rather than a threat.

Yet even the strongest mindset has to work a little harder in the body I live in. Having endometriosis adds an extra layer of complexity to serious endurance training. The inflammation, chronic pain, and affected energy levels, means every aspect of preparation – especially nutrition – becomes critical. Certain foods can trigger flare-ups, turning fuelling into both a necessity and a delicate balancing act. While training for the 80 km ultra the year prior, I consulted a sports dietitian. He recommended 30 g of carbs per hour and emphasised consuming carbs for the hour ahead. He also suggested alternatives to standard gels – something I was ready for. I experimented with jam sandwiches during long runs: simple, effective, and easy for my body to handle. I had to monitor my macronutrient balance carefully, however. I learned the hard way that too much healthy fat could trigger my endometriosis – abdominal pain striking in the early hours of the morning and disrupting my sleep. Managing my condition required constant adjustments, patience, and a willingness to try, fail, and try again.

Fuelling and mindfulness strategies helped, but balancing training with life – especially the social, sun-drenched pull of summer – was a challenge of its own. I wanted to push my endurance without sacrificing the activities that bring me joy. Training for a February event meant starting in October and pushing through the summer months. I love being on the water – wakeboarding, waterskiing, wakesurfing – and balancing the discipline of training with the joy of the season became its own kind of endurance challenge.

Back-to-back long runs were a vital part of my program, designed to replicate race conditions and originally scheduled for Fridays and Saturdays to accommodate work and study commitments. But as Mark and I spent more weekends away for water sports, my routine had to shift. Running long distances while away wasn't realistic – being on the water demanded both energy and time, and combining it with long runs was too much. So I moved my long sessions into weekdays, sometimes waking at 4 am to run before farm work, computer work, or study. When needed, I'd split sessions between morning and night. The hardest part wasn't always the training itself – it was not wanting to miss out on any part of my life.

Eight weeks out from the event, during the Christmas/New Year period, we headed to Gol Gol, New South Wales, on the Murray River, with friends. The days were warm and slow – early mornings on the water, and long afternoons on the riverbank. Even with the relaxed pace, I stayed mindful: moderating alcohol, eating well, and avoiding overload. My knees were already close to their limit, and every choice mattered.

Then, on the final day of the trip, I injured myself in the most ridiculous way. I pulled the nose of our wake boat toward me to leap onto it, but as I launched, the boat rebounded, the rope it was tied to snapped tight, and I fell straight onto the taut rope. The impact hit my right groin. The ache was immediate and unforgiving. I assumed it was a deep bruise and rested, knowing I had a 15 km run scheduled for the next morning.

By evening, bruising had already begun to spread. Still, at 4:30 am, I laced up and headed out. I'd been squeezing longer runs into early mornings so I could still enjoy the water and time with friends. Balancing holiday relaxation with water sports and strict training sometimes felt like juggling too many balls at once.

The moment I started running, the pain was sharp and immediate. Most of the route was bitumen and concrete, so I shifted onto grass when I could. By the time I reached the town of Mildura, the pain was intense – especially each time I pushed off from the traffic lights. Still, I kept going. Unless I was close to collapsing, stopping was never an option. I could walk if needed, but the 15 km had to happen.

A couple of weeks after the accident, test results revealed that the gracilis tendon in my right leg had partially torn, pulling fragments from the pubic bone. With the event only four weeks away – and just two weeks of intense training left – I leaned on the advice of those around me to work out a strategy. The expertise of my personal trainer, GP, and massage therapist merged with my own stubborn determination to keep going.

Despite the persistent pain in my right groin, I chose to stick to my training plan, modifying whatever I needed to. It was a familiar negotiation, much like living with endometriosis – learning how to persist through pain in order to keep showing up. I adapted where I could: adjusting weights and exercises, shifting my run–walk ratios, cycling instead of running, swapping rest days and listening carefully to what my body would allow.

Wakeboarding wasn't ideal. It added an unnecessary load – but I loved it too much to give up. Being behind the boat on glassy water at sunrise or sunset held its own kind of magic: the smooth glide of the board, the warmth of the air, the mesmerising stillness. I couldn't let that go either. So I modified that too – shorter sessions and fewer jarring movements, just enough to stay connected to the joy of it.

In the final weeks of training, frustration set in as my injury imposed constant limitations. It became a daily battle. Even routine tasks – feeding horses or checking water troughs – required forethought to avoid placing unnecessary strain on my body. When the frustration threatened to overwhelm me, I reached for something familiar. I leaned into principles from mindfulness and acceptance-based therapy – something I'd explored in a research project at uni on performance enhancement in athletes. I observed my frustration without judgement, acknowledged the discomfort, and kept redirecting myself to what I *could* control. Mindfulness eased the struggle, but it was the discipline I'd developed over years – through study, structure, and managing endometriosis – that truly carried me. Adapting wasn't new to me; it was something I'd done constantly throughout my life, learning to accept situations for what they are while finding ways to keep moving forward.

Mentally, I was ready, and aside from my groin and dodgy knees, I felt fitter than ever. My VO_2 max (the maximum amount of oxygen your body can use during intense exercise) was the highest it had ever been – "superior" for a female my age. I felt strong. Still, I knew how brutal ultra-distances can be. There's always a point when the mind asks: *Why did I pay to do this?*

To prepare for those moments, I asked friends to suggest songs for a supporters' playlist – something to keep me going in the mountains when things got tough. Mountain running is quiet, isolating, and demands self-generated encouragement, and collecting songs felt like bringing my friends along with me. The final playlist was a mix of R&B, rock, dance, and pop – each track carrying a connection. A close friend of mine, Ryan, created a separate playlist called *Beccy's Bangers* – two and a half hours of music made just for my run. It was such a thoughtful gesture, and I really appreciated the effort he'd gone to just for me.

I listened to both playlists during my three-hour drive to the high country, and they did exactly what I hoped: they filled me with energy, nostalgia, and a sense of support. I knew who had suggested each song, and thinking of them made me feel less alone in what I was about to do. By the time I arrived, I was buzzing – ready for my biggest challenge yet.

TEN

THE LONGEST RUN

THE 100 KM CHALLENGE I'D SIGNED up for wasn't just a race; it was an alpine odyssey. A single loop through the Victorian high country, beginning and ending on top of Mt Buller, climbing 10 peaks, passing eight historic huts, and stacking up more than 5,700 m of elevation. Known as Australia's toughest 100 km trail event, it demands not only endurance and navigation but the sheer will to keep moving through terrain capable of breaking even the strongest runners. Mt Buller had almost broken me once before. But this time, it wasn't just about conquering the mountains – it carried purpose too, raising money for early-intervention programs supporting children on the autism spectrum.

Given the event was held at the height of summer, I assumed the weather would be warm, dry, and relatively stable. Even in the mountains, where temperatures sit slightly cooler, I expected mild days in the low- to mid-20s and plenty of sunshine. Like most participants, I trained in the heat to acclimatise, preparing my body for long, exposed ridgeline sections.

In the days before the event, I packed all my mandatory gear and camping equipment – every item as compact and lightweight as possible. A volunteer group would transport my tent, mattress, and sleeping bag to a remote campsite for the overnight stop after day one, sparing me from carrying them during the run – but I still had to carry everything else. And the mandatory list was extensive: waterproof and windproof jacket, pants and gloves, thermals top and bottom, polar fleece, beanie, a map, course notes, compass, lighter, whistle, basic first aid kit, including a snake-bite bandage, a bivvy sack (a lightweight, waterproof cover that keeps you warm and dry outdoors), phone and battery pack, headtorch, sunscreen, food, two litres of water capacity, plus a waterproof bag to keep everything dry. This was the most remote event I'd ever attempted, and safety meant preparing for the possibility that help could take hours to reach me. The last thing anyone needed was dangerous weather – but that's exactly what rolled in.

The forecast deteriorated a few days prior: storms, heavy rain, freezing temperatures, and even snow. Snow – in the middle of summer, at a time when we're usually worried about catastrophic bushfires. It was an unprecedented weather event. I felt for the organising crew; an event this remote takes enormous planning. With near-zero temperatures predicted, runners camping in exposed alpine terrain, and sections crossing open ridgelines, safety became a genuine concern.

Two days out, the organisers made the difficult decision to reroute the entire event. They had to take down all the course markings they'd spent days setting up and designed two new routes – one for day one and a different one for day two – both starting and finishing in Mt Buller village. No remote camping – instead, I suddenly needed a hotel room. A bed. A roof. A hot shower. Unexpected luxury. Yes,

I was disappointed that the original course I'd trained so hard for was no longer possible, but attempting it in those conditions could have ended badly. They had every reason to cancel, but instead they worked tirelessly to salvage the event.

When I arrived at Mt Buller, nerves tightened as I looked out at the surrounding peaks. In my room, I laid out my gear and checked the list again – and again – because if anything was missing, I wouldn't be allowed to start. I'd triple-checked before leaving home, knowing there were no shops nearby to replace anything.

I headed to the village for the official gear check, got signed off, and returned for an early dinner before the race briefing. With severe weather expected, hearing the updated safety plan was crucial. The organisers handled it brilliantly, pulling together a last-minute adjustment that kept us safe while keeping the event alive. I didn't mind the changes at all – I was simply grateful to be there, ready to run.

The briefing emphasised just how harsh day two could be. Staying dry and warm would be essential – a lesson I'd learned the hard way years before. I reminded myself not to skip digging through my pack for extra gear, even if it felt inconvenient. Experience had taught me this wasn't the type of event for shortcuts.

I had an early dinner: spaghetti bolognaise – a carb-heavy meal I'd brought from home – eaten cold, since my room had no microwave, washed down with a generous handful of M&Ms. Then I went to bed early, hoping to soak up as much sleep as possible.

Day one
When my alarm sounded at 3 am, I rose immediately, took a hot shower to loosen my muscles, and began preparing. I RockTaped

every vulnerable spot – knees, feet, hips, collarbone, even my abdomen – to prevent rubbing, add support, and boost circulation. I covered my toes with Band-Aids to avoid blisters, wore my best socks, pulled on my knee sleeves, and layered up against the early-morning cold. With my body ready, I finished packing my running vest – with a litre of water and my GoPro – and did a thorough double-check of every item.

My pack weighed about 4 kg. Not much for most people, but with my 45 kg frame, carrying it across rocks, ridgelines, climbs, descents, and river crossings, I felt every gram. I paused in silence to mentally check in. How was I feeling? Nervous? Excited? Overwhelmed? All three, intensely. And yet, running through it all was something stronger: determination. A mindset focused on finishing, no matter what. Training had tested me in every way – pushing through pain, building strength, showing up on days I felt empty. Now, I was ready to give it everything.

At 4:45 am the village buzzed with energy – solo runners, two-day teams, three-day trekkers gathering in the dark. At the start line, everything becomes a mental game. Thinking about running 100 km was too overwhelming, so I relied on what always worked: breaking distances into smaller fragments. The countdown began, the crowd shifted, and suddenly we were off, running toward the Mt Buller summit.

Running in total darkness with only a headtorch is deceptively difficult. Shadows cast by runners behind you distort the trail, making it hard to read the terrain. If someone came close, I'd step aside out of courtesy – some passed, some didn't. I wasn't focused on speed; I was focused on surviving the kilometres ahead. The trail was littered with crevices, rocks, and holes. Every step demanded full attention.

Around 20 km, on the way to Craigs Hut, I didn't feel right. Maybe altitude. Maybe my body was warning me the way it sometimes does with endometriosis. I was nauseous and off, but not under-fuelled; I had kept on top of my hydration and food consumption. I slowed to a walk, alternating running and walking until I reached Craigs Hut. Fog hung thick in the air. I had to decide quickly: stop for a medic or refuel and keep moving. I chose to refuel. A volunteer handed me salt-and-vinegar chips and a can of Coke – pure magic. Within 20 minutes, my energy surged. From then on, that combination became non-negotiable at every checkpoint.

One of the greatest parts of endurance events is the camaraderie. I kept crossing paths with another runner – sometimes I caught him, sometimes he caught me. We chatted here and there, no obligation to stay together, yet our paths kept converging. Around 40 km in Mirimbah Valley, we met again at an aid station before the brutal climb back up Mt Buller. He grabbed an icy pole; I inhaled chips and Coke. We joked with volunteers about continually finding each other. We left the aid station together, and a few metres up the trail, a black snake crossed the track – a reminder to stay alert.

The climb was punishing. Head pressed down, quads burning, and fatigue tightening its grip. The higher we climbed, the rockier and steeper it became. The views were spectacular, but the exposure was unnerving. With a weighted backpack, I used three points of contact when climbing rocks, moving only when I felt secure. I paused at a rocky escarpment, breathless yet captivated. Mountains stretched endlessly, valleys plunged deep, birds soared effortlessly – such contrast to my laboured ascent. Then I looked ahead and saw the pink trail markers going straight up the rock face, with tiny figures crawling across the ridge. The climb ahead was monumental. My heart sank a little. Why had I signed up for this? I laughed, seeing the humour in it all. Holy moly. I was a sucker for punishment – but what a bloody adventure.

Reaching the end of day one was an enormous achievement. The final climb was merciless, leaving a mark on every runner who tackled it, and the next day, it was all anyone could talk about. That night, back in my hotel, my right knee was aching badly. I tried everything – hot towels, massage and rest. I'd lost most cartilage years ago and relied on a knee band and RockTape for support. With another 50 km to go on day two, I worried how I'd get through. But I had trained way too hard to stop now. I wasn't about to quit. I took a hot shower, washing the grime from my body and easing the tightness in my muscles. Dinner was early, takeaway from a pub in Mt Buller village. My body was spent; the day's run and relentless climbs had taken a huge toll. I couldn't help but wonder how I was going to summon the strength to do it all again the next day.

Day two

I woke at 3 am again, sore but determined. I meticulously taped my feet, ankles, calves, quads, collarbone, and abdomen. Running another 50 km felt impossible, so I broke it down into micro-steps: walk downstairs. Get to the start. Show up. That alone is a victory. At the start line, layered against the cold, I chatted with an older gentleman about how mad we were for doing this again. His knees were giving him grief too. The conversation steadied my nerves.

At 5 am we began, heading uphill toward the summit. The route dropped down the back of Mt Buller and onto a long and technical rocky escarpment, where loose rocks, uneven footing, and steep exposure left no room for error. Navigating that terrain in daylight is tricky; doing it in the dark with a headtorch demanded total focus. My right knee felt every downhill step. Anyone who gained on me, I stepped aside to let pass.

Eventually, I reached a ridge just as the sun rose. I paused to soak it in and take photos. It was breathtaking. The descent continued – nonstop, with no reprieve – and by the time I hit the valley, my right knee was screaming. At the aid station, there were no chips or Coke, so I grabbed what I could and continued.

The trail followed a stunning river. I stopped often for photos, backtracking for better shots. My mind drifted to the river crossings ahead – 21 in total. I knew how poorly my body coped with cold, and with snow forecast on the peaks later, today would be a test. But I had a plan: spare socks in my pockets with hand warmers, ready to keep my feet toasty. I couldn't change them until the final crossing, but if it didn't work, I could use my endometriosis heat belt to warm my feet. I was already wearing it under my running gear. Having two plans gave me confidence.

The river crossings were spectacular. Water rushed over rounded rocks, surrounded by bush and towering mountains. Depths varied – most mid-calf, a few mid-thigh. Currents weren't strong, but the deeper crossings threw me off balance as I picked my way across slippery rocks. After each crossing, the squelch in my runners was undeniable. My feet stayed cold, and just as they began to warm, another river appeared. By this point, running was limited. The outside of my right knee throbbed with every step. The pain and slow pace made it clear that power walking was the smarter option – conserving energy while avoiding further strain. Frustrating, yes, but if that's what it took to reach the finish line, that's exactly what I was going to do.

After the second-last river, I paused at an aid station for some salt-and-vinegar chips and a can of Coke before pressing on. When I reached the final river crossing, the trail pitched almost vertically. I found a log, sat down, and changed into fresh, warm socks, preparing myself for the climb ahead. By the time I resumed the climb, circulation had returned, and everyone ahead of me and behind me was puffing and climbing higher into the mountains. The next 20 km was when my supporters' playlist kicked in. The terrain climbed relentlessly, and with roughly 70 km behind me, my mood began to sink. I was exhausted, with the kind of exhaustion where you could sleep upright. Trudging along a dusty dirt road, legs burning, I'd glance up only to feel dread at the elevation ahead.

But each song brought someone with it. I pictured the person who chose it walking beside me, offering encouragement in their own voice. *What would they say right now? How would they say it? What would they tell me if I told them I wanted to give up?* Those imagined conversations carried me – step by step – making the impossible feel just a little more doable.

Music wasn't just comfort; it was chemistry. My brain's reward system was kicking in, releasing dopamine (feel-good hormones) with each familiar rhythm or lyric – lifting my mood, fuelling my motivation, turning exhaustion into focus. I repeated mantras too: *You are strong. You can do this. The finish line won't come to you, you have to get there yourself.*

The runner from day one kept appearing, and on the brutal hill climbs, we mostly stayed side by side – sometimes talking, sometimes silent. We arrived at the final aid station together, and just as we got there, the weather turned. Rain swept sideways, temperature plummeting. Hyperaware of my core temperature, I pulled on extra layers. A kind volunteer handed me a toasted sandwich and Coke served in a medieval-looking mug he'd found somewhere in the hut. I was so grateful for his hospitality. The rain eased slightly, and I set off again.

But soon it returned – relentless, icy, unforgiving. *Get comfortable being uncomfortable*, I reminded myself. As I drew closer to Mt Buller, the fog thickened, the wind increased, and the rain cut like ice. I was layered head to toe: two sets of thermals, running sleeves, long-sleeve top, fleece jumper, windproof and waterproof jacket, pants and gloves, and a beanie. Moving efficiently in all that gear, through fog and freezing rain, was a battle. Crossing under an unused ski lift, I laughed. Me – the one who hates the cold, who wears a hoodie when everyone else is in shorts – trudging through extreme conditions in a voluntary endurance challenge I had willingly signed up for.

The ski fields were exposed, wind whipping sideways, visibility almost zero. I angled my body to shield myself from the weather, but with no shelter, I was completely exposed. Then the icy rain turned into snow. Rounding a few corners, I stumbled upon brief pockets of shelter from the wind. I paused, took it all in, and couldn't help but laugh at the absurdity of it: me, running a 100 km race in near-Antarctic conditions. I snapped a few photos, recorded some videos, and let Ryan's playlist fill my ears, using the surge of dopamine to push me forward. When "Take It Off" by Fisher & Aatiga – a dance track – came on, I pictured another close friend, David, nicknamed Diesel for his full-throttle, give-it-everything energy, performing his signature dance moves on the boat during our long summer afternoons. The memory made me laugh, transporting me far from the biting cold. For a moment, I imagined the hot sun on my skin and the freedom of gliding across glassy water – a vivid contrast to the icy snow and whipping wind.

Eventually, I reached a car park, completely disoriented. Exhausted, aching, unable to spot the next marker. A medic in a 4WD honked. "Are you okay?" she asked. In my head: *No.* Out loud: "Yes." "You're nearly there. One more climb to the summit, then it's all downhill." Everything in me wanted to stop. But I hadn't come this far to quit. I had just 10 km to go.

The summit was brutal – ice and wind stinging my face, visibility near zero. But music anchored me. "One Night in Bangkok" by Murray Head played as I forced myself up the summit. That song will always take me back to that exact moment: exhausted, frozen, and quietly amused at the absurdity of it all.

At the summit, I tore a page from a book in the tub – proof of completion I'd made the final climb – fingers numb through gloves. The book's title escaped my attention. The descent was agony; knees, hips, feet, groin, toes – everything – ached. But the finish line pulled me onward. I continued on, already feeling relief that the finish line was close.

And then, finally, the village appeared. Snow was falling. The air was 0 °C, though it felt closer to -6 °C. The finish line came into view, and I ran across the village square, passing under the arch – earning a buckle and medal that felt like solid, shining proof of every punishing step it had taken to get there. Inside, I warmed up and watched other runners finish in the snow, still barely believing what I had just done. I waited for my torn page to be carefully framed by the event organisers – a small monument to the final, gruelling climb. I messaged my friends and Mark to tell them I'd made it – their pride and excitement matched the disbelief I felt myself. All I wanted then was a hot shower, a hearty meal, and a bed – simple comforts that had never felt more deserved.

The next morning, I was sore but intact. After climbing nearly 6,000 m over 100 km in two days, it felt nothing short of miraculous. I packed up, drove down the mountain, and stopped in Mansfield for a burger and a Coke. I devoured it.

The page I tore from the summit book now sits framed on my shelf at home. Fittingly, it was the front page of Chapter 13, about a girl arriving at a homestead after riding through river crossings, on a mare – a female horse. I own three mares myself, and I was also the 13th female to cross the finish line. Whether coincidence or not, it felt like a small, perfect alignment.

ELEVEN

TRAIL-LIFE LESSONS

EVERY STEP ON THE TRAIL has its lesson, and life has a way of reflecting it back. Patience, for example, is learned on endless climbs when the summit seems impossibly far – and it carries over to life, whether waiting for recovery after surgery or managing the daily unpredictability of endometriosis. Endurance is forged through hours of running over rocky ridges and single trails, but it's the same endurance that keeps me moving through chronic pain, or days when even simple tasks feel impossible. Resilience is tested when my legs burn, my knees ache, and the weather turns against me – but it's the resilience I call on when setbacks happen off the trail, when complications arise, or when progress feels painfully slow. Courage shows up in the quiet moments too: leaning into the pain of a steep, endless climb, knowing each step forward is a choice to keep going despite exhaustion, or daring to face another day of uncertainty and discomfort, despite fatigue.

The lessons from the trail and life feed each other. Every hill I've climbed has taught me to slow down, breathe, and trust my strength – just as every medical setback has taught me to listen, adjust, and keep moving forward. Step by step, whether on the mountain or through the challenges of a body that doesn't always cooperate, I've learned that patience, endurance, resilience, and courage are not abstract ideals – they are practices, lived and refined through every challenge I face.

Practising key principles: lessons for life and endurance:

- **The power of incremental progress.** No one begins endurance running by starting with 100 km events. Capacity builds one step at a time. Training taught me that progress is rarely dramatic – it's a quiet accumulation of small, consistent efforts. Life mirrors this truth: confidence, strength, and resilience grow through repeated, modest successes. Study taught me the same lesson. I didn't suddenly become capable of understanding complex ideas or managing heavy workloads; I built that capacity gradually, one subject, one assignment, one late-night effort at a time. Whether rebuilding strength after surgery, pacing myself through a challenging week, or slowly moving through grief, incremental progress became my anchor.

- **Learning to live with discomfort.** Endurance running is uncomfortable. So is living with endometriosis. Yet both taught me that discomfort doesn't always signal danger – it can be a space for growth. Rather than resisting it, I learned to move with it, to stay present even when it was hard. Training my body to handle physical strain mirrored training my mind to handle emotional ones, building distress tolerance and patience.

- **Preparation and consistency.** Races are won long before the start line. It's the months of early mornings, sore muscles, and deliberate planning that make endurance possible. Life demands the same approach: preparation matters. Structuring my days with rest, nourishment, and recovery in mind helps me conserve energy for what mattered most – study, work, and connection. That discipline that carried me through managing chronic illness became a blueprint for long runs.

- **Listening to my body – with strategy and respect.** Endurance sports demand careful attention to subtle signals. Ignore fatigue for too long, and the body rebels. I learned to read these messages – Am I fuelled sufficiently? Is my training sufficient? – and respond accordingly. Life, and illness, required the same mindfulness. I learned to distinguish between discomfort I could push through and pain that demanded a pause. Listening to my body wasn't weakness – it was strategy. That awareness became the foundation for sustaining health and balance over the long term.

- **Self-compassion and mindset.** Not every run goes as planned, and not every day with endometriosis does either. Some challenges are unexpected, testing patience and perseverance in equal measure. Learning to meet those moments with kindness rather than frustration became essential. Self-compassion – treating myself with the same understanding and care I would offer a friend – helps me stay motivated and emotionally steady. Resilience isn't about being perfect; it's about returning to myself with gentleness, no matter how many times I stumble.

- **Embracing uncertainty.** On a trail, weather, terrain, and unexpected obstacles force adaptation. Life mirrors this unpredictability – illness flares, plans change, and outcomes aren't guaranteed. Staying flexible and moving forward despite uncertainty builds courage and resilience. The more I embraced life's unexpected turns, the better I managed the unknown on the trail.

- **Patience with progress.** Endurance events show that improvement is incremental. Life mirrors this: recovery, learning, and personal growth don't happen overnight. Trusting the process, showing up consistently, and celebrating small victories became key. Each tiny improvement on the trail reminded me of the patience needed for gradual recovery beyond it.

- **Courage in small moments.** Bravery isn't only about grand gestures – it's lining up for your first race unsure if you can finish, or tackling a long run when every step aches. Life asks for the same quiet courage: facing another medical treatment, standing up for my needs, or simply taking the next step when fear or fatigue looms.

- **Focus and presence.** Trail running demands full attention – one misstep can be costly. Life, especially managing chronic illness, benefits from the same focus: being present in the moment, noticing my body, and making intentional choices. Learning to keep my mind on the immediate first step, rather than the entirety of a daunting distance, became invaluable in both arenas.

- **Community and support.** On long runs, camaraderie – fellow runners, volunteers, cheering strangers – is invaluable. Life mirrors this: leaning on others, asking for help, and sharing my journey strengthens resilience and motivation. Support transforms struggle into connection, making challenges feel manageable rather than insurmountable, especially during times of loss.

- **Gratitude in struggle.** Even when the trail is punishing, moments of beauty – a sunrise, a river crossing, or the scent of mountain air – bring joy. Life is similar: noticing small moments of comfort, love, or achievement helps sustain me through hardships. Gratitude became a compass, keeping me grounded even in the toughest conditions.

- **Mental flexibility.** Plans rarely go perfectly. Weather, terrain, and unexpected obstacles taught me to adapt. Life demands the same: learning to pivot, problem-solve, and let go of rigid expectations is essential for long-term endurance. Flexibility isn't surrender – it's survival.

- **Celebration of completion.** Finishing a hard trail run is tangible proof of perseverance. Life often lacks clear finish lines, but taking time to acknowledge effort, even in small wins, reinforces resilience and motivation. Every day, every step forward, becomes worth celebrating.

- **Honouring limits.** Knowing when to rest, refuel, or pause – even when every instinct pushes you forward – is part of endurance. When I injured my groin, I couldn't keep training as usual. I had to adapt my gym workouts, swapping exercises and reducing weights to not aggravate the injury. Life, too, teaches that ignoring limits can be costly. Recovering from double jaw surgery and navigating the loss of my mum showed me the physical and emotional toll of pushing past my boundaries. I had to pay attention to regulating my nervous system to function normally again. Listening to my body and recognising boundaries is an act of courage, not weakness.

- **Finding joy in the process, not just the outcome.** Trail running can be brutal, yet the journey itself – learning, discovering, moving – holds value beyond the medal. Life mirrors this: growth and resilience come not just from achieving goals, but from embracing the process, step by step, moment by moment.

- **Comparison: the mind's detour.** On the trail, it's easy to glance at another runner and feel behind, slow, or less capable. In life, especially with chronic illness, comparison can be just as distracting and discouraging. I learned that the only meaningful measure is my own pace – honouring my limits, celebrating small wins, and focusing on personal growth. Comparing myself to others only drained energy that could be spent doing something more meaningful. Both on the mountains and in life, staying in my own lane keeps me resilient, motivated, and fully present.

- **Reframing success.** Over time, I began to recognise the value of reframing success. On the trail, success might mean crossing a finish line, or even just showing up in the first place, willing to give it a go. In daily life, it might mean simply showing up – cooking a meal, finishing a uni assignment, or taking a walk. Drawing from psychology, I began reinforcing these "small wins" to build self-efficacy: the quiet belief that I could influence my circumstances, even when life felt hard or uncertain.

• **Adaptation.** Through all of this, I came to understand that endurance – whether physical or emotional – isn't about pushing through pain at all costs. It's about adapting. It's learning when to rest, when to persist, and how to find meaning in the process itself. The same mindset that carried me through ultramarathons – incremental effort, mindful awareness, preparation, and compassion – became the framework for navigating the complexities of endometriosis and beyond. In many ways, my identity as an athlete and as someone living with chronic illness converged. Both journeys demanded the same fundamental qualities: patience, self-awareness, and the courage to keep moving forward, even when the path was steep, uncertain, or painfully slow.

Through all these lessons, I came to see that the trail is a mirror for life. Every climb, every river crossing, every aching step has a lesson waiting if I take the time to notice it. And just as the mountains test me physically, life tests me emotionally, mentally, and spiritually. There have been days when grief and loss weighed heavily – loss of time, loss of health, even the quiet grief that comes with watching others live lives my body doesn't always allow. On the trail, the mountains don't wait, the river doesn't pause, and the weather doesn't soften because I'm struggling. And in life, nothing pauses for my pain either. The key is to keep moving forward.

I've learned that patience is more than just waiting – it's a willingness to engage fully with the present moment, whether that moment is a long, steep climb or a difficult day managing endometriosis. Endurance is not just physical stamina; it's the quiet persistence of showing up for myself when every cell in my body is begging me to stop. Resilience isn't simply bouncing back – it's learning to absorb the challenges, integrate them, and emerge stronger, more aware, and more compassionate toward myself.

One of the most important realisations from running and life is that suffering is not a measure of failure – it is a teacher. The trail exposes me to brutal weather and rocky ridges, where one wrong step could be fatal. In life, I've faced setbacks, medical procedures, and unexpected flare-ups that tested the limits of my endurance. Both demanded that I slow down, observe, and respond with intention rather than impulse. Both taught me that struggle is part of growth, and that embracing it with awareness and care can transform pain into insight.

I've also learned that resilience is rarely a solitary act. Even the toughest ultramarathon is supported by volunteers, friends, and fellow runners. Similarly, navigating chronic illness is not meant to be done alone. Seeking support, accepting help, and sharing both triumphs and hardships create a network of strength that multiplies the courage and endurance within me. Life, like a long trail, is rarely linear. There are twists, setbacks, and moments when the path disappears entirely. And yet, in those moments, the skills honed on the mountains – self-compassion, focus, flexibility, and patience – become lifelines.

Finally, I've discovered that joy and gratitude are not found only at the summit or the finish line – they are present in every step of the journey. A quiet sunrise, the sound of a river, the laughter of a friend, or the warmth of a hot meal after a long day – all these moments are evidence that progress and beauty coexist with struggle. Life and trail alike remind me that the process is as important as the outcome. The act of moving forward, however slowly or imperfectly, is a triumph in itself.

In the end, what I carry away from the mountains is not just medals, records, or kilometres – it's a mindset, a way of being. It is the understanding that life, like a trail, is rarely predictable, often uncomfortable, but endlessly rewarding for those willing to engage fully. And so, I keep moving, step by step, heart open, mind present, and courage steady – because whether on the trail or in life, the journey itself is where we truly find strength and meaning.

PART FIVE

ANCHORS

TWELVE

JOY

JOY ISN'T SOMETHING THAT ARRIVES fully formed; it's something we learn to notice, protect, and nourish in the small moments that make life feel worth living. Research shows that tending to our own needs lowers stress and protects us from burnout, creating space for lightness, energy, and emotional spaciousness. By prioritising my wellbeing, I began treating joy not as something accidental, but as something I could actively cultivate. And considering Joy is my middle name, it feels fitting in how I live my life.

Still, joy isn't always obvious. Sometimes we don't yet know what gives us that spark, and curiosity becomes part of the journey. I've learned through exploration, trying new things, and by paying attention to the moments that shift my energy and lift me up. Joy reveals itself in layers, and as we grow and change, the shape of our joy evolves with us.

But what does joy feel like in everyday life? For me, joy is something that fulfils my soul – quietly, deeply, without needing explanation or justification. It's often something simple, almost ordinary, that fills me with good energy. Take calm water, for example. I can't really explain why it affects me the way it does, but it gives me an immediate sense of peace, safety, and stillness. My whole nervous system settles. That's why I love paddleboarding – the soft glide of the board, the warm sun on my body, the gentle sound of water moving beneath me. It's undemanding, quiet, and grounding. Particularly when it's just me on the water among nature.

Water sports bring me the same kind of joy – with more energy, adrenaline, and laughter. I first learned to ski in my mid-thirties, and over time I ventured into wakeboarding and wakesurfing, each of which has its own rhythm and thrill.

Beginner waterskiers often start with two skis until they find their balance. Once comfortable, many move to a single ski, known as slalom skiing, which allows for sharper turns and faster carving. Wakeboarding, by contrast, uses a single board with both feet strapped in, letting you carve, jump, and ride the wake – part snowboarding, part surfing. Wakesurfing is different again. You start with a rope, but once you're riding the boat's wave, you let go and flow freely, almost as if you're surfing in the ocean. It's about rhythm, balance, and the feel of the water beneath your feet – a movement that's both exhilarating and meditative. Each sport offers a distinct challenge and sensation, yet they all capture the skill, focus, and joy of moving gracefully across the water.

Growing up, I didn't have access to these activities, so it was all entirely new when I came to it in adulthood. At first, it was incredibly frustrating. Learning water sports is hard – especially when you don't own a boat. You spend most of those rare times on the water falling, face-planting, getting water up your nose, and nursing sore muscles. Meanwhile, your friends are laughing at your spectacular wipeouts, entertained by the last 20 minutes of your struggles. There's honestly nothing immediately enjoyable about it. But sometimes joy isn't found immediately.

For me, it emerged slowly, from persistence – gradually feeling less frustration, laughing at myself, and experiencing the thrill of doing something challenging well enough to have fun. That sense of progress, no matter how small, was satisfying. It taught me early on that effort itself can be its own reward, and that even in moments of struggle, there is something energising in continuing. It was that experience that reminded me how much persistence matters – and why I was willing to keep going, even when it was difficult.

Persistence isn't just a personality trait – it's a skill shaped by motivation, meaning, and the belief that effort leads to improvement. Research on grit and growth mindset shows that when a goal matters to us and feels connected to the person we want to become, we're far more likely to push through discomfort, frustration, and repeated setbacks. That's exactly what kept me going with water sports.

At the same time, my goals in sports have never been about being the best. I don't chase podiums or try to outperform others; I simply want to do things well enough to enjoy them. As an adult, I noticed that many people seemed driven by the need to prove themselves, to achieve mastery, or to measure success against others. I realised that comparing myself to them only drained my energy – energy I'd much rather invest elsewhere. When I was learning to waterski, I fell constantly, swallowed half the lake, and felt clumsy far more often than capable. And still, the simple desire to improve – just a little each time – and chase the desire to reach the fun stage created its own momentum. Every small gain reinforced the understanding that the effort was worth it, activating my brain's reward systems and making persistence feel not only possible but meaningful. Over time, those hard lessons became undeniable proof that confidence grows through challenge, not ease.

Wanting to be "good enough" at something rather than the best is not a flaw – it's a deeply healthy, well-researched mindset in psychology. Self-determination theory shows that we thrive when an activity meets three core needs: autonomy (choosing it freely), competence (feeling capable), and relatedness (feeling connected). For me, especially in my hobbies, the goal isn't mastery or comparison – it's reaching a level of competence that lets me feel confident, present, and fully engaged. That's what creates intrinsic motivation: the desire to do something simply because it feels meaningful or enjoyable, not because it earns a podium or outperforms anyone else. Water sports taught me this clearly. In the beginning when I fell constantly, I wanted to feel capable enough to actually enjoy it, which carried me through all the frustrating, humbling lessons. Once the skills stop feeling impossible, the nervous system settles, fear softens, and enjoyment becomes available. I don't need perfection for joy – just enough ease and flow to participate wholeheartedly.

You've probably heard the saying "a jack of all trades but master of none". That's how I often see myself – someone who can do many things, just not exceptionally well. And honestly, I'm perfectly at peace with that. Studying psychology has helped me understand that not everyone is driven by competition. For some of us, striving to be "the best" creates pressure that actually drains the pleasure out of the experience. Doing things well enough to have fun allows for challenge without overwhelm, growth without self-judgement, and expression without the constant weight of comparison. It leaves room for curiosity, joy, and a more sustainable kind of engagement – the kind that makes you feel alive rather than evaluated. That is, without question, who I am.

Combining my love for calm water with water sports really hits my sweet spot. Much like paddleboarding, gliding across glassy water on skis or a wakeboard is indescribable – the sensation of skimming effortlessly over the smooth surface, and riding the rhythmic rush beneath your feet is exhilarating and grounding at the same time. It's like moving in perfect harmony with the water, fully immersed in the moment, with every sense alert yet relaxed, and nothing else in the world demanding attention. Add hot weather, the company of friends, and I'm instantly transported to that place of pure energy and presence.

Because for me, water sports isn't just about the water – it's the people. Long weekends away with friends, the downtime between rides, the laughter and music that fills the boat, the easy conversations about life's challenges, the quiet comfort of simply being in each other's company. I'm lucky: the people in my life are genuine, kind, and have a great sense of humour. We don't take ourselves too seriously and we laugh a lot when we're together. Mark and I spend a lot of time with Ryan and Diesel – holidays, weekends away, even a month-long road trip through the USA. We have a rhythm that works: we can tap out when needed, be honest, tease each other, and navigate the highs and lows as a team.

My friendships with those who I grew up with – Julie, Tamara, Sarah and Chris – are different but an equally meaningful kind of joy. I've known Julie and Sarah since primary school and Tamara and Chris since kindergarten. We've gone through all our schooling together. We're in our mid-forties now, and the comfort level is effortless. We can go weeks or months with little contact, then fall straight back into connection as though no time has passed. I've watched them move through relationships, children, career changes, and the unexpected curveballs of adulthood. What I value most about them is their authenticity and acceptance. Over time, I've realised that I'm drawn to people whose values mirror my own – kindness that softens the edges of the world, acceptance that makes us feel safe exactly as we are, humility that enables us to embrace our place without needing to dominate, empathy that allows us to truly understand one another, presence that makes conversations feel alive, authenticity that invites honesty, and compassion that reminds us we're all human. These qualities are the foundation of the friendships I cherish. Good friendships are rare, and I don't take mine for granted.

In much the same way, travel has become another enormous source of joy – something I never could have imagined as a child. Coming from a low socioeconomic background meant that my holidays were occasional, small and practical. My first flight was at age 20, not long after I met Mark. We travelled to Port Douglas in Queensland. From there, the world slowly opened. Vanuatu was my first overseas trip, and since then I've travelled to more than 25 countries, and a lot of Australia too, mostly with Mark or for work. Mark and I have snorkelled reefs in the Pacific, been on safari in South Africa, explored the Greek Islands, wandered through Switzerland's mountains, and swum under waterfalls in places that felt like a dream.

South Africa was especially unforgettable. We stayed in open-air huts where encounters with scorpions and monkeys were real possibilities. At night, a guard with a gun escorted us back to our room because of roaming wildlife – buffalo in particular. Being charged by one was a very real threat. Lying in bed, listening to lions in the distance – their deep, rhythmic calls – was captivating. From the lodge's viewing deck, we watched buffalo bathe at the watering hole, and I embraced every photographic opportunity: cheetahs, zebras, giraffes, rhinos, lionesses with their cubs, even a lion feeding on a carcass. The elephants, though, captivated me most. Watching them roam the plains, I was struck by their blend of strength and calm, their deep social bonds, and the way they moved with such presence. Perhaps I could relate, understanding the importance of herd dynamics as I had with horses.

As part of our trip, our host dropped us off at a treehouse miles from camp. We climbed in, were given a pick-up time, and left to observe whatever unfolded on the vast African plain. A few animals came and went, but what stayed with me wasn't what I expected. The weather, predicted to turn, did so spectacularly. From the treehouse, we watched dark clouds roll across the plains, lightning flashing intermittently and low, rumbling thunder echoing in the distance. The warm evening air pressed gently against my skin, carrying the subtle scent of the earth. It was one of those once-in-a-lifetime moments, the kind that etches itself permanently into my memory.

In a different but equally meaningful way, spending time with family in the UK created memories I still hold close. Not long after Dad passed away, Alana, Mark, Mitchell (Alana's partner at the time) and I travelled to the UK to spend time with family. We stayed with Dad's sister, Mary, and her husband, Bill, who cooked us a fry-up each morning – bacon, eggs, and sausages. We visited cousins and second cousins, some of whom I'd never met before in person. I felt deeply supported and loved, particularly given the timing. Being surrounded by so many relatives was wonderful, though at times overwhelming – I wasn't used to such a large family. I loved our shared sense of humour, so like Dad's and mine, and hearing the English accents around me made things feel familiar and comforting, as did discovering parts of England that held connections to Dad. After that, Alana, Mark, Mitchell, and I continued our journey with a tour across Europe, carrying with us the warmth and memories of family.

Over time, I've realised that it's the company, more than the destination, that can leave the longest imprint. The month-long trip across the USA with Mark, Ryan, and Diesel was unforgettable – not just for the places I saw, but for the people I was with. We travelled the California coast from Santa Monica to Huntington, explored Mexico, Big Pine, Yosemite National Park, Las Vegas, Zion National Park and Lake Powell, collecting stories and shared moments. Every destination left its own impression, but Yosemite National Park was on an entirely different level. The sheer scale of the landscape was overwhelming – towering granite cliffs and cascading waterfalls. Hiking through the valleys, standing at the edge of cliffs, and looking up at the sky framed by the iconic El Capitan and Half Dome filled us with awe. The light and shade on the rock faces, the clear rivers, vast valley views and fresh mountain air created a feeling that stayed with us long after we left. Yosemite wasn't just a place – it was an experience that reminded me of the power of nature and the quiet, humbling joy of full presence. Sharing it with the people I did made it even more special.

Travel, I've learned, is full of contrast. Some experiences lift your spirit, while others reveal the struggles people face. Driving past sprawling slums in South Africa, where poverty seemed to stretch endlessly, left an imprint. I remember feeling quite taken back at the sight: a vast landscape dotted with thousands of makeshift shelters built from corrugated iron, scrap wood, and plastic sheets. Narrow, dusty pathways wound between crowded homes. Scattered rubbish and debris littered the ground, and the heat and dust seemed to hang heavy over the settlement. The sheer density, the improvisation of daily life, and the visible struggle of survival were impossible to ignore. It's hard to accept that in our modern world, such extreme poverty still exists. In Indonesia, I witnessed similar struggles: communities lacking basic infrastructure and families making do with what little they had. That sense of hardship took on an even heavier weight in Rwanda, where visiting the Genocide Museum brought a physical ache, a gut-wrenching confrontation with the depths of human suffering. These experiences, across continents, deepened my understanding of global inequality and expanded my gratitude for the life I live. Travel expands your view of the world, forcing you to see life through perspectives you might never encounter at home. It nurtures gratitude for the privileges we often take for granted, while deepening empathy for those whose circumstances are so different. These experiences changed the way I see things – not just the world, but the people around me, and even myself – teaching me humility, compassion, and the quiet power of awareness.

At home, Mark and I have a giant world map on our loungeroom wall – a pinboard that marks every place we've visited – an idea I borrowed from Dad. I remember his map of Melbourne in our back room when I was a child, dotted with red pins marking every job he'd completed. Our map does more than track travel; it sparks conversation with guests about places they've been, where we've been, or the destinations we dream of exploring. There's something quietly joyful about standing in front of it, tracing routes with your eyes, imagining past adventures and future journeys – it turns the world into a tangible, living story.

That same sense of joy threads through another lifelong companion: music. Like travel, it has the power to transport me – lifting me back to childhood memories, carrying me through the present, and sparking excitement for what's yet to come. I've turned to it in moments of deep emotional hurt, shared it alongside friends, and used it to energise myself during training and running events.

I began learning music in my early thirties, when Mark gave me an acoustic guitar for my birthday. Learning, however, was harder than I expected. I felt clumsy and doubted I'd get anywhere at first. After a few lessons, I realised that playing well comes down to consistent practice. I fit it in wherever I could – between work, study, and other commitments. I've never aimed to be the best; I simply want to play well enough to enjoy it, to feel the music, and to share in the quiet, personal joy it brings. I had always been moved by the energy of someone playing and singing. Interestingly, joy isn't always something we generate on our own – sometimes it comes from the people around us. When I see someone fully committed, excited, or completely absorbed in what they're doing, it sparks joy in me as well.

Humans are highly social creatures, and much of our emotional experience is shaped by those around us. Psychology and neuroscience explain this through concepts like emotional contagion and mirror neurons. Emotional contagion is the unconscious process of mirroring another person's emotions – so when someone is genuinely joyful, enthusiastic, or calm, our brains tend to reflect that state, often boosting our own mood. Mirror neurons amplify this effect: observing someone experiencing positive emotions can activate our brain as if we were feeling it ourselves. This connection helps explain why joy can ripple outward – but it also highlights the difference between joy and happiness.

Happiness is a broader sense of wellbeing, often tied to life circumstances. But life is full of moving parts – small imperfections, unexpected challenges, and things completely outside our control that can throw a spanner in the works. Because of that, complete happiness is elusive. Joy, on the other hand, is immediate and present-focused. It can flicker to life even in the midst of struggle, offering a sense of aliveness and meaning.

Yet our sense of joy is often distorted by social media. We're constantly shown a highlight reel: perfect relationships, perfect holidays, perfect achievements, perfect lives. It's not intentional deceit – it's simply the culture. We share the shiny moments and tuck the hard ones away, and in doing so, we risk comparing our real, messy experiences to a filtered version of someone else's life.

I'm no different. My posts are filled with beautiful landscapes, holidays, horses, sunshine, water sports, and endless sunrises and sunsets. I don't upload the days when I'm exhausted, overwhelmed, doubting myself, or struggling with fatigue. But as more people open up about the realities behind their curated posts, it helps rebalance our expectations of what a good life actually looks like. Admittedly, my friends might look at my socials and assume I'm always out having fun, always thriving. That's not the case. Which is why what we see online should always be viewed through a cautious lens.

What I've come to realise is that joy isn't loud, perfect, or constant. It builds quietly, piece by piece – through the people you love, the places that move you, the moments that remind you who you are, and the small rituals that bring you back to yourself. It also requires intention: choosing to slow down, to care for yourself, and to create space between the demands of work, study, and life.

I've ignored that space before, and I know how easily joy can slip away when you do. I've been to the darkest corner a person can find themselves in, and I know how frightening, isolating, confronting, and incredibly hard it is to sit with suicidal thoughts. In those moments, the idea of finding your way out feels almost impossible.

But it *is* possible. It takes time, support, and incredible courage, but there is a way through – and I'm living proof of that.

What I've learned since then is that joy is often shaped by contrast. Psychology suggests that our emotional experiences work in relation to one another – without moments of pain, uncertainty, or loss, our nervous system has no reference point for what renewal and joy truly feel like. The hardest times don't just make the good moments sweeter; they help us recognise them, hold them, and let them matter. Joy becomes less about perfection and more about presence.

Practical takeaways:

- **Focus on what shifts my energy.** I take notice of what lifts me up and I make space for those activities, people, or environments that energise me.

- **Have something to look forward to.** It doesn't have to be a big event like an overseas holiday or weekend away – sometimes it's as simple as catching up with a friend or enjoying a midweek activity after work that offers anticipation and excitement.

- **Nurture good friendships.** I invest in relationships that are supportive, kind, and uplifting – they're essential for resilience and joy.

- **Experience life outside my own world.** Seeking new perspectives, adventures, cultures, and experiences beyond my routine broadens my understanding and reminds me to appreciate what I have.

- **My feelings of joy are valid on their own.** I honour what brings me joy without needing anyone else's permission or approval. I do the same for others, supporting what brings them fulfilment too.

- **See value in the hard times.** Challenges and setbacks aren't just obstacles – they provide context for the good moments. Without experiencing difficulty, it's hard to fully recognise and appreciate joy when it comes.

- **Fulfilling my soul isn't a task; it's a return.** To the parts of me that feel most alive, most honest, and most at home in the world. This is a safe, peaceful, sacred place, just for me.

THIRTEEN

HORSES

THERE'S SOMETHING ABOUT THE STEADY rhythm of hooves on a dirt road that draws me fully into the present, quieting my mind. For me, that sense of grounding arrived in the form of Elli, my first horse, who came into my life when I was 26 – just months before Dad passed away.

I had always loved animals, but horses were largely unfamiliar to me. Growing up, I had no real connection to horses beyond the occasional trail ride during school holidays. As an adult, though, I found myself drawn back to horse riding, often driving an hour to a small trail-riding business in the Reefton Spur, simply to spend time in the bush – reconnecting with the freedom and calm it always brought.

When the owner of the small trail-riding business decided to sell his horses due to rising insurance costs, I wondered: *Could I actually have a horse of my own?* When I mentioned the idea to Mark, predictably, he was not enthusiastic. "We're not getting a horse," he insisted. But I was determined. I dug through all my horse books, created a budget, researched local agistment options, and somehow – though I'm still not entirely sure how – I convinced him.

I remember the day we brought Elli home. We drove up to the Spur with Mark's parents' dog, Sophie – a fluffy white Lhasa Apso we were dog-sitting at the time. My cousin Tahlia came too. That clean, white dog rolled in horse manure while we were loading Elli into the float. The drive home was filled with the unmistakable smell of horse manure, and Sophie, proud as ever, was now decidedly less white.

Elli is a palomino Quarter Horse – quiet, gentle, and reserved. Only later did I realise how much trauma she likely carried from her early days as a broodmare. The scars on her hind legs hinted at hobbling, a harsh practice sometimes used in horse breeding to restrict a mare's movement by tying or binding her legs while humans introduce a stallion to mate with her. It can leave lasting physical and emotional scars, causing pain, stress, and long-term trauma.

Her emotions were subtle, almost hidden. Once I learned more about horse behaviour, I began noticing the tiniest signals: a faint twitch under her eye when she felt uncertain, sending her into a freeze rather than a flight response. She reminded me so much of myself, quietly internalising her feelings. She was wary of Mark and strangers alike. She relied on me to slow down, to meet her where she was. If I rushed, her trust would vanish.

She was excellent on the trails, and I rode her everywhere. Tahlia and I would go out together – one of us would ride while the other walked, then we'd swap – and the sound of Elli's hooves on a dirt road was almost hypnotic: steady, rhythmic, and calming. Being around her felt grounding, a connection that psychology helps to explain. A horse's nervous system is exquisitely attuned to subtle shifts in human emotion. Because they respond to the energy we bring into their space – calm, anxious, uncertain, or confident – they naturally invite co-regulation. Horses live entirely in the present moment. They're not planning tomorrow, replaying yesterday, or analysing their worth. And when you stand beside them, your body often begins to mirror that same presence. Research in equine-assisted therapy shows that time spent with horses can lower cortisol, slow breathing, and activate the parasympathetic nervous system – the system responsible for grounding, calm, and restoration. But beyond the science, it's the felt experience that matters: the slow rhythm of grooming, the warmth of their body beside yours, the quiet, wordless communication. Horses aren't interested in your job title, your to-do list, or the story you're currently telling yourself about how well you're coping. They meet you exactly as you are, and in doing so, they invite you to do the same. For me, spending time with horses feels like being anchored – pulled out of my head and back into my body, back into the moment, back into myself.

A few years after I got Elli, my life took an unexpected turn with Kansas – the Paint mare Mark and I rescued, who needed emergency surgery and months of rehabilitation. She is the opposite of Elli: confident, expressive, and remarkably clear in her communication. Today, she leads our herd at home with quiet authority. Without her, so much of my life would have taken a very different path: I likely wouldn't have studied equine science, volunteered in equine welfare, trained in equine podiatry, or started an agistment and education facility. Her presence set all of this in motion, shaping not just my career, but the way I experience and understand the world of horses.

Over the years, Tahlia and I shared some unforgettable rides together – her on Kansas, me on Elli – through bush trails, along quiet stretches of beach, and on weekend camping trips. But with horses, beauty and risk always coexist.

I broke my collarbone once when I was thrown from Elli after a dog spooked her. Years later, I came off her again on a dirt road – this time far worse. I was knocked unconscious, most of my top teeth were pushed backward, and one front tooth was completely knocked out. I always wore a helmet, and I hate to think what might have happened if I hadn't. Fortunately, Mark was with me, walking our dog Jet. He called an ambulance and, against the odds, managed to find my missing tooth on the dirt road.

In emergency, a nurse pushed my tooth back into my gum without anaesthetic. The pain was indescribable, and it was the first time I instinctively turned to visualisation – a technique where the mind creates controlled, calming scenarios to activate the brain's relaxation pathways and blunt the perception of pain.

Years earlier, as a young adult, I had invested in braces to straighten my teeth – a treatment my parents couldn't afford when I was growing up. To have all that time, effort, and expense undone was frustrating. A plastic surgeon stitched my face and tried to reposition my teeth manually. He did a reasonable job, but they were never quite the same.

I've broken a wrist too, simply by being in the wrong place at the wrong time – bowled over by a spooky horse at our agistment facility and landing with my hand outstretched. Experiences like these taught me that being vigilant around horses isn't optional; it's essential. They're grounding, healing, and extraordinary animals – but they also demand respect.

With those lessons in mind, I welcomed Sachie into our lives, my third mare. Gentle and intuitive, she has a softer presence that balances Kansas's boldness. She's a Clydesdale Warmblood cross, but, like Elli, she carries a cautiousness around humans that demands patience and trust to navigate.

When she first came into my care, she was difficult to catch and fearful when handled, often trying to flee. But once I earned her trust, I discovered how much she loves being scratched. She learned to point with her nose and teeth, guiding me to the exact spot she wanted touched. Our relationship has mostly been built on the ground. She can spook easily, and I didn't have the time or expertise to build her confidence under saddle, so instead we developed trust in quieter ways.

The fourth and final member of our herd at home is Hugo, who brings a completely different energy. He is a wise old Thoroughbred, well-respected within the group, and completely at ease among the mares. Hugo began his life as a racehorse, travelling to countries like Hong Kong. When I first opened our agistment facility in 2014, his owner, Rosie, contacted me to see if I would take him in – Hugo and Rosie were our first clients.

At his previous agistment, Hugo had been kept in a private paddock and labelled "dangerous" – anxious, prone to rearing, and considered impossible to handle. Rosie was at her wit's end, running out of options. Euthanasia was even being considered because selling him carried serious risks: if he ended up with the wrong person, he could injure someone, or himself, or be sent to the saleyards, where challenging horses are often bought for meat or resold, continuing a vicious cycle.

I began slowly, introducing him to my mares at our agistment facility. He stayed in his own paddock but could interact with them over electric tape, giving each horse space while they were still able to get to know one another – and allowing me to observe their behaviour. This is a strategy I use for integrating all new horses. I immediately noticed calm behaviours: sniffing, gentle squeals from the mares, mutual grooming, and a clear desire to be together. They would often congregate along the fence line, and if the mares walked away, Hugo would pace anxiously at being left alone. After a couple of days, the herd was merged.

Hugo's transformation was remarkable: he became calm, soft, and connected. He was a completely different horse. The herd played together, cantering across the wide-open paddocks, kicking their heels with excitement; they grazed side by side, slept and rested together, and groomed one another. Years later, they were moved from our agistment facility to our farm at home, where Hugo now enjoys a peaceful retirement.

Every day, he greets me with a gentle nicker – that soft, low, affectionate sound horses make when they recognise someone. He stands quietly at liberty to be rugged, often chooses to stay near me, and remains one of the sweetest and calmest horses I've ever known. A true gentleman, he has a place in my heart as if he were my own.

Watching Hugo and the mares interact highlights just how central natural social behaviours are to horses. As highly social herd animals, they rely on instinctive patterns of communication, hierarchy, and movement for survival and wellbeing. Herds provide protection – multiple eyes and ears increase vigilance and allow threats to be detected early – while established social structures reduce conflict and help individuals predict each other's behaviour, lowering stress.

Observing subtle cues – a flick of an ear, a gentle nudge, or a shift in posture – reveals a sophisticated language of connection and intention. Horses engage in grooming, where they nibble and scratch each other's coats with their mouths, as well as synchronised movement and social learning. These behaviours strengthen bonds, reduce anxiety, and help regulate emotions, demonstrating how naturally attuned they are to one another. Isolation, by contrast, can elevate stress hormones, raise heart rate, and even trigger behavioural problems – as Hugo so clearly demonstrated. Living in a stable social group promotes calmness, resilience, and opportunities for learning, underscoring that social connection is not just a preference – it is a biological necessity. By understanding and respecting these instincts, humans can build trust, encourage wellbeing, and foster genuine, reciprocal relationships with horses.

Running a herd-only agistment facility taught me just how complex this becomes when you layer human personalities, business logistics, and horse behaviour on top of one another. Herd dynamics are predictable in theory, but in practice they can be challenging – different owners with different expectations, horses with distinct temperaments, different horses coming and going, geldings gelded late who still behave like stallions, and mares in and out of season all influence how the group functions. Ensuring safety for both humans and horses is a constant balancing act, requiring problem-solving, honest communication, and adaptability. It isn't easy – but easy has never been my goal. My aim has always been to allow horses to live as naturally as possible: in herds, with space, companionship, and the freedom to be horses. Honouring their instincts in this way supports both their physical and emotional wellbeing.

Despite the constant work, seven days a week – the feeding, rugging, hoof trimming, managing herds, rotating paddocks, weed spraying, fencing – horses bring me joy. They remind me to breathe. To slow down. To pay attention to my energy, my body, my presence. They help me process emotions without saying a word. On warm evenings, I sometimes sit in the paddock and watch Hugo and the mares graze and intermittently groom each other, observing the quiet interactions of herd life. If they choose to walk over and be with me, I enjoy their presence. If not, I'm content simply sharing their space.

Horses have taught me more than I ever expected – about behaviour, emotion, connection, boundaries, and trust. They've shaped how I move through the world and understand myself. I sometimes wonder if my psychology training could merge more intentionally with my horse world – perhaps through equine-assisted therapy, using the natural sensitivity and social intelligence of horses to support human emotional growth.

Horses mirror our emotions, respond to our energy, and provide immediate, non-judgemental feedback, helping people develop self-awareness, emotional regulation, and confidence. Working alongside horses often teaches patience, presence, and the value of clear, honest communication – skills that translate directly into everyday life. For me, the intersection of human wellbeing and equine behaviour represents a natural progression of my personal and professional journey and has increasingly shaped my interest in trauma recovery.

In practice, supporting a traumatised horse demands patience, compassion, and humility. Through this process, powerful insights emerge about connection, safety, and resilience – lessons that translate meaningfully to human healing. You see how trauma lives in the body – through a flinch, a freeze, a brace, or a refusal – not defiance but memory. Slowly, with steadiness and calm, the horse softens, engages, and offers something fragile and extraordinary: their trust.

Trust with a horse cannot be demanded; it is earned through consistency, safety, and gentle presence. Approaching quietly, respecting personal space, and responding calmly to cues signal reliability and security. Over time, these small, thoughtful behaviours allow a horse to relax, engage, and offer attention willingly. Research shows that horses are highly sensitive to human body language, tone, and energy, reflecting our emotional state and responding best to calm, confident, and empathetic handling. In learning to earn a horse's trust, humans cultivate mindfulness, patience, and emotional attunement – skills that strengthen not only the human–horse bond but also our capacity for empathy in everyday life.

There is something profoundly healing about earning the trust of an animal who has every reason not to give it. Trauma leaves its mark, yet when fear is met with patience and care, it can soften into curiosity, as can mistrust into connection, and guardedness into playfulness. Watching a horse roll in the grass, nuzzle a companion, or chase a big ball with unrestrained delight is a gentle but powerful reminder that life is not only about survival or productivity – it is about presence, trust, and joy.

These moments of play show that healing isn't always serious or structured. Curiosity, laughter, and lightness are just as essential as discipline and care. For us as adults, allowing space for play nurtures creativity, eases stress, and reconnects us to a sense of freedom we often forget. In sharing these playful moments with horses, I'm reminded that growth and recovery are found not only in effort and endurance, but also in the simple, joyful, unguarded experiences that invite us back into connection.

Horses remain one of the purest sources of joy in my life – steady, grounding, and honest. Working with them has shown me that even the most wounded souls can learn to trust, to feel valued, and to be truly seen. It's a powerful reminder that empathy, consistency, and presence aren't just tools for horses – they are tools for every relationship in life.

Lessons from horses and life:

- **Trust is earned, not demanded.** Trust grows slowly through consistent, thoughtful actions – listening to and observing a horse's signals, respecting their space, and demonstrating reliability day after day. These principles apply equally to life: in running, I build trust in my body; in managing endometriosis, I learn which strategies help and which don't; in study or work, following through on commitments shows consistency and dependability. Small, steady actions like these lay a foundation of trust – in myself, in others, and in the world around me – that deepens and strengthens over time.

- **Presence matters.** Horses respond instantly to energy, body language, and focus. Being mindful, calm, and attentive fosters connection and emotional attunement. In life, this translates to showing up fully – for yourself, for others, and for the moments that matter most, whether that's a long training run, a challenging work project, or a quiet evening with loved ones.

- **Trauma leaves marks, but healing is possible.** Past experiences – abuse, neglect, illness, or loss – shape behaviour and perception. Gentle, consistent care and self-compassion allow trust, confidence, and resilience to return. Healing is rarely linear, but with patience and care, trust and resilience can gradually be restored – both in the horse and in ourselves.

- **Empathy and emotional regulation are learned through interaction.** Observing and responding to a horse's subtle cues improve self-awareness and emotional intelligence. Similarly, facing personal hardships, helping others through grief, or pacing myself through an ultramarathon teaches me to pay attention, control my reactions, and respond with intention rather than impulsively.

- **Play is essential.** Horses naturally engage in play, which promotes mental and physical wellbeing. Adults benefit too: allowing space for curiosity, laughter, and joy – even amid life's challenges – reduces stress and reconnects us to vitality. Play reminds me that resilience is built not only through effort and endurance but also through lighthearted fun.

- **Connection and boundaries go hand in hand.** Respecting a horse's space and signals is crucial for safety and trust. Learning to set and honour boundaries translates into healthier human relationships too, whether with friends, partners, colleagues, or even myself. Boundaries are an act of care, not isolation.

- **Healing is incremental.** Progress often comes in small steps. With handling traumatised horses, chronic illness, grief, or long training runs, small, consistent efforts accumulate into transformation.

- **Joy can be found in simplicity.** Horses teach me to slow down, notice the present, and find satisfaction in small, grounding experiences. Amid life's chaos – whether coping with illness, juggling responsibilities, or pushing through the final kilometres of a race – pausing to breathe, connect, and appreciate simple moments restores energy and perspective.

- **Making a difference matters.** Witnessing how human-centred the equine industry can be inspired me to create change – to give horses more freedom, dignity, and choice. Starting my own business allowed me to offer an environment that prioritises their wellbeing, teaching me that meaningful impact comes from intentional action. This lesson extends beyond horses: observing where strategies or systems fall short, and taking deliberate action to improve them – whether for animals, people, or myself – creates ripples of positive change that reach far beyond the immediate moment.

- **Tools don't equal power; liberty reveals the truth.** I've learned having the latest equipment, gadgets, or control methods doesn't create trust or connection with horses. True insight comes when an animal is given freedom to move, choose, and respond naturally. It is in that freedom that their true personality, needs, and emotions emerge. The same applies to life: authority, status, or resources alone do not foster respect, understanding, or genuine connection. It is through granting space, autonomy, and freedom – both to others and myself – that authenticity and real growth emerge.

- **Knowledge is power.** The more I learned about what is important to horses – and not what's convenient for me – the deeper my understanding and connection became. Observing their behaviour, studying their needs, and understanding their natural instincts allowed me to communicate more clearly, respond more empathetically, and create an environment that truly supports their wellbeing. This lesson goes beyond horses: by moving beyond my own agenda to truly understand the perspectives, needs, and experiences of others, I can cultivate deeper relationships, greater empathy, and more meaningful connections in every area of life.

FOURTEEN

INTEGRATION

Looking back, the thread running through every challenge – endometriosis, ultrarunning, career, study, volunteering, grief, and surgery – is resilience. But resilience isn't a single skill; it's a framework shaped by many experiences, each adding depth, strength, and perspective.

Running taught me the power of incremental progress, mental endurance, and pushing past perceived limits. Living with chronic illness refined my self-compassion, pacing, and ability to listen to my body while still moving toward my goals. Balancing work, study, and volunteering built discipline, time management, and practical problem-solving. And grief, loss, and physical trauma strengthened my emotional regulation and capacity to recover.

These experiences became building blocks of:

- **Physical resilience** – undertaking endurance training, understanding my body's limits, and learning recovery strategies.

- **Emotional resilience** – navigating setbacks, stress, and grief while remaining functional.

- **Cognitive resilience** – applying reflection, planning, and problem-solving to complex challenges.

- **Purpose-driven resilience** – pursuing work, volunteering, and study aligned with my values.

- **Relational resilience** – cultivating trust, empathy, and connection through people and horses alike.

By weaving these threads together, I developed a mindset that balances challenge and care, action and reflection, effort and rest. Resilience is not about perfection or invincibility – it's a practice, a living architecture. Life's curveballs are unpredictable, and each challenge demands its own response. Resilience has given me a way to stay grounded when the world tilts. It has taught me to make space for discomfort without being consumed by it, and to trust that I can navigate whatever arrives, even if I've never walked that exact path before.

Through this lens, resilience is not simply surviving – it is intentionally living, learning, and shaping a life aligned with values, curiosity, and compassion. It is a skillset, a mindset, and an ongoing practice, available to anyone willing to engage fully with life's challenges and lessons.

I hope that by sharing my journey, you can take something away to apply in your own life. Resilience is not reserved for those who are "naturally tough". It is cultivated intentionally, in small daily choices: choosing self-compassion over self-criticism, presence over distraction, curiosity over fear, and action over stagnation.

Think about the obstacles in your own life – the moments that felt impossible or unfair. Each one carries a lesson if you allow it. From chronic illness, you may learn to listen to your body and respect your limits. From grief, you may discover how to sit with discomfort while still seeking light. From work, study, or volunteering, you may cultivate discipline, focus, and purpose. And from relationships, human or animal, you may discover empathy, patience, and the power of connection. All of these experiences are building blocks for resilience – each one strengthens your capacity to meet the next challenge with courage.

Life will always be challenging. There will be moments when you feel powerless, exhausted, or unsure. But every past experience – every hardship, setback, or loss – has prepared you in ways you may not even realise. Even if it doesn't feel like it, you have built skills, learned lessons, and strengthened capacities that will support you through whatever comes next. Resilience is like a muscle: it grows each time you face discomfort, choose action over surrender, and make space for self-compassion alongside perseverance. Trust that the strengths you need are already within you – and remember, you don't have to do it alone. Reach out, seek guidance, and utilise the people, tools, and resources around you; they are there to help you navigate the challenges ahead.

Final thoughts:

- **Apply skills across domains.** Lessons from one area of life can strengthen another. Applying the same strategies in new situations builds a toolkit of transferable skills that can be drawn upon whenever life presents something unfamiliar.

- **Practise self-reflection.** Regularly assess what's working, what needs adjustment, and how challenges shape growth. Explore thoughts, feelings, and reactions to experiences, noticing patterns and insights. Reflections help us understand ourselves better, make intentional choices, and strengthen the skills and habits that support resilience.

- **Anchor yourself in purpose.** Pursuing what truly matters can open doors to opportunities that naturally align with your goals and passions. When your actions align with your values, motivation becomes more sustainable, and even difficult days take on a sense of purpose.

- **Recognise progress over perfection.** Resilience is built gradually, and every challenge is part of the ongoing process of learning, adapting, and strengthening.

- **Create safety and trust in relationships.** Learning to build trust fosters deeper connection and emotional security. It is earned over time through consistency, honesty, and reliability – both in how we show up, how we respond to others and how others respond in return.

- **Allow joy and playfulness.** Even in the face of adversity, making room for joy and playfulness restores energy and perspective. Notice what energises you, and pursue it freely, without waiting for anyone's approval.

- **Honour incremental growth**. Change and healing rarely happen quickly; patience and persistence are key.

- **See obstacles as opportunities**. Every challenge, no matter how small or overwhelming, contains a lesson. Setbacks are not signs of failure – they are opportunities for growth.

- **Channel your energy**. Focus on what you can control. Let go of what you can't.

- **Celebrate incremental progress**. Pause to recognise and enjoy the small victories along the way; meaningful change unfolds gradually.

- **Cultivate presence and empathy**. Listen, observe, and respond – not just to others, but to yourself. Awareness of patterns, needs, and emotions builds resilience.

- **Invest in self-care**. Our health is the foundation for everything else. Embrace lightness, curiosity, play, and laughter. It connects us to a sense of freedom and joy.

- **Trust the process**. Healing and transformation are rarely linear. Some days feel stagnant; others surprise you with breakthroughs. Both are part of the journey.

- **Feed your soul**. Do what makes you feel alive. This space is entirely yours. Claim it, protect it, honour it.

Your story, like mine, will be unique. I invite you to take what resonates from my journey and apply it to your own. Lean into life fully, face challenges step by step, reflect on setbacks, practise self-compassion, embrace discomfort as a teacher, and align effort with purpose. Notice moments of joy and connection amid difficulty – they are signs that growth is happening. Trust that your body, mind, and spirit are capable of more than you realise. Every step toward understanding yourself, nurturing meaningful connections, and living intentionally strengthens your resilience.

You have the power to rise, adapt, and thrive. The tools are already within you, shaped by your experiences. Let this be your permission to move forward courageously, to grow with curiosity, and to live life beyond limits.

ACKNOWLEDGEMENTS

I **WANT TO THANK EVERYONE** who has supported me on this journey – through the challenges of chronic illness, the highs and lows of training and endurance, my career and educational pursuits, the loss of both my parents, and the process of writing this book.

To my family, friends and colleagues, who listened, cheered, and believed in me even when I doubted myself. Each of you have shaped my journey in your own way – through encouragement, laughter, or simply being present. I am endlessly grateful for the lessons, love, and light you have shared, which have carried me through every challenge and triumph.

To the mentors who offered guidance and insight along the way, whose wisdom and honest feedback helped me navigate challenges, grow in confidence, and see possibilities I might never have imagined. I'll be forever grateful to you for taking me under your wing, seeing my potential, and encouraging me to trust myself.

To the incredible health and wellness professionals – sports physiotherapist, massage therapist, osteopath, podiatrist, dietician, naturopath, personal trainer, and GP – who shared their knowledge, supported my training and recovery, and inspired me with their dedication and expertise. You were patient and accepting of my stubbornness, always helping me find a way to achieve my goals despite chronic health challenges, ailments, and injuries.

I've come to believe that the universe has a way of unfolding life exactly as it should – not in rigid detail, but with a rhythm and purpose that we often can't see in the moment. Nearly every person I've crossed paths with in my life has taught me something, whether through support, challenge, or even contrast. There's a quiet magic in recognising that nothing is truly random: the people, experiences, and even the hardships all play a part in guiding us, teaching us, and helping us grow.

Finally, to you, the reader – thank you for walking this path with me. I hope these pages inspire and encourage you, reminding you that growth, resilience, and joy are always possible, even amid life's challenges. You already hold the power to shape your wellbeing in ways that feel nourishing and true to you.

REFERENCES

The information in this book is supported by peer-reviewed research, including the following scientific journals and studies.

Chapter One: Unmasked

Jain, S., & Dalton, M. E. (1999). Chocolate cysts from ovarian follicles. *Fertility and Sterility, 72*(5), 852–856. https://doi.org/10.1016/S0015-0282(99)00367-2

Chapter Two: Diagnosis

Greene, A. D., Lang, S. A., Kendziorski, J. A., Sroga-Rios, J. M., Herzog, T. J., & Burns, K. A. (2016). Endometriosis: Where are we and where are we going? *Reproduction, 152*(3), R63–R78. https://doi.org/10.1530/REP-16-0052

Haydardedeoglu, B., & Zeyneloglu, H. B. (2015). The impact of endometriosis on fertility. *Women's Health, 11*(5), 619–623. https://doi.org/10.2217/whe.15.48

Kodete, C. S., Thuraka, B., Pasupuleti, V., & Malisetty, S. (2024). Hormonal influences on skeletal muscle function in women across life stages: A systematic review. *Muscles, 3*(3), 271–286. https://doi.org/10.3390/muscles3030024

Nezhat, C., Agarwal, S., Lee, D. A., & Tavallaee, M. (2022). Can we accurately diagnose endometriosis without a diagnostic laparoscopy? *Turkish-German Journal of the Gynecological Association, 23*(2), 117–119. https://doi.org/10.4274/jtgga.galenos.2022.2022-2-2

Chapter Three: Science Behind the Symptoms

Arab, A., Karimi, E., Vingrys, K., Rezaei Kelishadi, M. R., Mehrabani, S., & Askari, G. (2022). Food groups and nutrients consumption and risk of endometriosis: A systematic review and meta-analysis of observational studies. *Nutrition Journal, 21*(58). https://doi.org/10.1186/s12937-022-00812-x

Babic, T., & Browning, K. N. (2014). The role of vagal neurocircuits in the regulation of nausea and vomiting. *European Journal of Pharmacology, 722,* 38–47. https://doi.org/10.1016/j.ejphar.2013.08.047

Bjorkman, D. J. (1998). The effect of aspirin and nonsteroidal anti-inflammatory drugs on prostaglandins. *The American Journal of Medicine, 105*(1, Suppl. 2), 8S–12S. https://doi.org/10.1016/S0002-9343(98)00069-2

Della Corte, K. W., Perrar, I., Penczynski, K. J., Schwingshackl, L., Herder, C., & Buyken, A. E. (2018). Effect of dietary sugar intake on biomarkers of subclinical inflammation: A systematic review and meta-analysis of intervention studies. *Nutrients, 10*(5), 606. https://doi.org/10.3390/nu10050606

Ghoreishy, S. M., Hashemi Javaheri, F. S., Ghasemisedaghat, S., Noormohammadi, M., Eslamian, G., Kazemi, S. N., & Rashidkhani, & B., Taheripanah, R. (2025). Alternative healthy eating index may predict a reduced odd of endometriosis: Results from a case-control study. *BMC Women's Health, 25,* 249. https://doi.org/10.1186/s12905-025-03805-0

Layunta, E., Buey, B., Mesonero, J. E., & Latorre, E. (2021). Crosstalk between intestinal serotonergic system and pattern recognition receptors on the microbiota–gut–brain axis. *Frontiers in Endocrinology (Lausanne), 12,* 748254. https://doi.org/10.3389/fendo.2021.748254

Liang, Y., Xie, H., Wu, J., Liu, D., & Yao, S. (2018). Villainous role of estrogen in macrophage-nerve interaction in endometriosis. *Reproductive Biology and Endocrinology, 16*, 122. https://doi.org/10.1186/s12958-018-0441-z

Machairiotis, N., Vasilakaki, S., & Thomakos, N. (2021). Inflammatory mediators and pain in endometriosis: A systematic review. *Biomedicines, 9*(1), 54. https://doi.org/10.3390/biomedicines9010054

Shigesi, N., Harris, H. R., Fang, H., Ndungu, A., Lincoln, M. R., The International Endometriosis Genome Consortium, The 23andMe Research Team, Cotsapas, C., Knight, J., Missmer, S. A., Morris, A. P., Becker, C. M., Rahmioglu, N., & Zondervan, K. T. (2025). The phenotypic and genetic association between endometriosis and immunological diseases. *Human Reproduction, 40*(6), 1195–1209. https://doi.org/10.1093/humrep/deaf062

Sumbodo, C. D., Tyson, K., Mooney, S., Lamont, J., McMahon, M., & Holdsworth-Carson, S. J. (2024). The relationship between sleep disturbances and endometriosis: A systematic review. *European Journal of Obstetrics & Gynecology and Reproductive Biology, 293*, 1–8. https://doi.org/10.1016/j.ejogrb.2023.12.010

Tarjanne, S., Ng, C. H. M., Manconi, F., Arola, J., Mentula, M., Maneck, B., Fraser, I. S., & Heikinheimo, O. (2015). Use of hormonal therapy is associated with reduced nerve fiber density in deep infiltrating, rectovaginal endometriosis. *Acta Obstetricia et Gynecologica Scandinavica, 94*(7), 693–700. https://doi.org/10.1111/aogs.12652

Wald, A., Van Thiel, D. H., Hoechstetter, L., Gavaler, J. S., Egler, K. M., Verm, R., Scott, L., & Lester, R. (1981). Gastrointestinal transit: The effect of the menstrual cycle. *Gastroenterology, 80*(6), 1497–1500. https://doi.org/10.1016/0016-5085(81)90263-8

Velho, R. V., Taube, E., Sehouli, J., & Mechsner, S. (2021). Neurogenic inflammation in the context of endometriosis – what do we know? *International Journal of Molecular Sciences, 22*(23), 13102. https://doi.org/10.3390/ijms222313102

Velho, R. V., Werner, F., & Mechsner, S. (2023). Endo belly: What is it and why does it happen? – A narrative review. *Journal of Clinical Medicine, 12*(22), 7176. https://doi.org/10.3390/jcm12227176

Wei, Y., Liang, Y., Lin, H., Dai, Y., & Yao, S. (2020). Autonomic nervous system and inflammation interaction in endometriosis-associated pain. *Journal of Neuroinflammation, 17*(1), 80. https://doi.org/10.1186/s12974-020-01752-1

Xie, M., Qing, X., Huang, H., Zhang, L., Tu, Q., Guo, H., & Zhang, J. (2025). The effectiveness and safety of physical activity and exercise on women with endometriosis: A systematic review and meta-analysis. *PLoS ONE, 20*(2), e0317820. https://doi.org/10.1371/journal.pone.0317820

Ye, C., Chen, P., Xu, B., Jin, Y., Pan, Y., Wu, T., Du, Y., Mao, J., & Wu, R. (2023). Abnormal expression of fission and fusion genes and the morphology of mitochondria in eutopic and ectopic endometrium. *European Journal of Medical Research, 28*, 209. https://doi.org/10.1186/s40001-023-01180-w

Chapter Four: Mind–Body Connection

Aboushaar, N., & Serrano, N. (2024). The mutually reinforcing dynamics between pain and stress: Mechanisms, impacts and management strategies. *Frontiers in Pain Research, 5*, 1445280. https://doi.org/10.3389/fpain.2024.1445280

Becker, S., Gandhi, W., & Schweinhardt, P. (2012). Cerebral interactions of pain and reward and their relevance for chronic pain. *Neuroscience Letters, 520*(2), 182–187. https://doi.org/10.1016/j.neulet.2012.03.013

Machairiotis, N., Vasilakaki, S., & Thomakos, N. (2021). Inflammatory mediators and pain in endometriosis: A systematic review. *Biomedicines, 9*(1), 54. https://doi.org/10.3390/biomedicines9010054

Maddern, J., Grundy, L., Castro, J., & Brierley, S. M. (2020). Pain in endometriosis. *Frontiers in Cellular Neuroscience, 14,* 590823. https://doi.org/10.3389/fncel.2020.590823

Pasternack, S., Suvilehto, J., Härkki, P., Heikinheimo, O., Sipilä, R., & Kalso, E. (2025). Pain, emotions, interoception, and bodily sensations in patients with endometriosis. *European Journal of Pain, 29*(10), e70144. https://doi.org/10.1002/ejp.70144

Tang, Y., & Tang, R. (2024). Health neuroscience – How the brain/mind and body affect our health behavior and outcomes. *Journal of Integrative Neuroscience, 23*(4), 69. https://doi.org/10.31083/j.jin2304069

Chapter Five: The Architecture of Childhood

Dewberry, C., Juanchich, M., & Narendran, S. (2013). Decision-making competence in everyday life: The roles of general cognitive styles, decision-making styles and personality. *Personality and Individual Differences, 55*(7), 783–788. https://doi.org/10.1016/j.paid.2013.06.012

Nagy, E., Pilling, K., Watt, R., Pál, A., & Orvos, H. (2017). Neonates' responses to repeated exposure to a still face. *PLoS ONE, 12*(8), e0181688. https://doi.org/10.1371/journal.pone.0181688

Maudgil, S. (2024). Effects of childhood trauma on brain functioning. *International Journal of Interdisciplinary Approaches in Psychology, 2*(4), 328–338. https://psychopediajournals.com/index.php/ijiap/article/view/199

Vella, S.-L. C., & Pai, N. B. (2019). A theoretical review of psychological resilience: Defining resilience and resilience research over the decades. *Archives of Medicine and Health Sciences, 7*(2), 233–239. https://doi.org/10.4103/amhs.amhs_119_19

Chapter Six: Knowledge is Power

Colman, D. E., Echon, R., Lemay, M. S., McDonald, J., Smith, K. R., Spencer, J., & Swift, J. K. (2016). The efficacy of self-care for graduate students in professional psychology: A meta-analysis. *Training and Education in Professional Psychology, 10*(4), 188–197. https://doi.org/10.1037/tep0000130

Chapter Seven: Grief

American Psychiatric Association. (2013). *Diagnostic and statistical manual of mental disorders* (5th ed.). American Psychiatric Publishing, p. 53.

Coates, T. J., & Thoresen, C. E. (1978). What to use instead of sleeping pills. *Journal of the American Medical Association, 240*(21), 2311–2312. https://doi.org/10.1001/jama.1978.03290210093042

Chapter Eight: Honouring the Good Days

Paley, C. A., & Johnson, M. I. (2025). Human resilience and pain coping strategies: A review of the literature giving insights from elite ultra-endurance athletes for sports science, medicine and society. *Sports Medicine, 55*, 2137–2146. https://doi.org/10.1007/s40279-025-02277-4

Thornton, O. R., Ly, S., Colón, I., Cole, H., & Li, W. (2023). The psychological indicators of success in ultrarunning – A review of the current psychological predictors in ultrarunning. *Annals of Medical and Health Sciences Research, 13*(7), 730–736. https://doi.org/10.5281/zenodo.17090729

Chapter Twelve: Joy

Deci, E. L., & Ryan, R. M. (2017). *Self-determination theory: Basic psychological needs in motivation, development, and wellness.* Guilford Press, p. 95.

Lam, K. K. L. & Zhou, M. (2025). A meta-analysis of the relationship between growth mindset and grit. *Acta Psychologica, 255,* 104872. https://doi.org/10.1016/j.actpsy.2025.104872

Procházková, E., & Kret, M. E. (2017). Connecting minds and sharing emotions through mimicry: A neurocognitive model of emotional contagion. *Neuroscience & Biobehavioral Reviews, 80,* 99–114. https://doi.org/10.1016/j.neubiorev.2017.05.013

Chapter Thirteen: Horses

Baldwin, A. L., Walters, L., & Rector, B. K. (2023). Effects of equine interaction on mutual autonomic nervous system responses and interoception in a learning program for older adults. *People and Animals: The International Journal of Research and Practice, 6*(1). https://doi.org/10.56631/paij.v6i1.3

Cooper, J. J., & Mason, G. J. (1998). The identification of abnormal behaviour and behavioural problems in stabled horses and their relationship to horse welfare: A comparative review. *Equine Veterinary Journal Supplement, 27,* 5–9. https://doi.org/10.1111/j.2042-3306.1998.tb05136.x

Earles, J. L., Vernon, L. L., & Yetz, J. P. (2015). Equine-assisted therapy for anxiety and posttraumatic stress symptoms. *Journal of Traumatic Stress, 28*(2), 149–152. https://doi.org/10.1002/jts.21990

Torres Borda, L., Auer, U., & Jenner, F. (2023). Equine social behaviour: Love, war and tolerance. *Animals, 13*(9), 1473. https://doi.org/10.3390/ani13091473

Bᴇᴄ Fʟᴀsᴇʏ ɪs ᴀ Mᴀsᴛᴇʀ of Professional Psychology student, endurance athlete, and passionate advocate for individuals navigating chronic illness. Having lived with undiagnosed endometriosis for more than 20 years, she intimately understands the physical, emotional, and social challenges of persistent pain, fatigue, and the frustration of navigating a healthcare system that often struggles to recognise complex conditions. Her lived experience fuels her empathy and informs her approach to supporting others facing similar journeys.

Bec draws on her personal journey, professional training, and extensive experience as an endurance athlete to explore resilience, mindset, and practical strategies for overcoming obstacles. Through ultra-trail running, she has honed lessons in patience, perseverance, and incremental growth – principles she applies to both life and wellbeing. Her work integrates insights from psychology, sport, and lived experience, offering guidance and inspiration to those confronting physical, mental, or emotional challenges.

Outside of her professional and athletic pursuits, Bec finds grounding and joy in spending time with her horses, whose subtle intelligence and social nature continually teach her about trust, connection, and presence. She is also deeply committed to initiatives that promote wellbeing, empowerment, and personal growth, believing that even small acts of support and encouragement can have profound ripple effects.